REBIRTHING
MADE EASY

by
Colin P. Sisson.

i

TOTAL PRESS

© COPYRIGHT 1985 by Colin P. Sisson

All Rights Reserved

ISBN 0 9590014 0 9

First Edition March 1985
Second Edition May 1985
Third Edition February 1987
Fourth Edition May 1988
Fifth Edition April 1990

All enquiries about Rebirthing or for obtaining copies of this
book, write to:

COLIN P. SISSON
P.O. Box 7264
Wellesley Street,
AUCKLAND 1
NEW ZEALAND.

Printed in Singapore by
Singapore National Printers Ltd

ACKNOWLEDGEMENTS

Frank Smith — Who proof read a large part of this work, and with his wit and inspiration, made a major contribution to the production of this book. Thanks Frank.

Chris Lewton — Who proof-read portions of the work, and with his gift of words and sentence structure, was able to guide me through the difficult 'mine fields' of the English Language. Thanks Chris.

Leonard Orr and Sondra Ray — For their kind permission to use extracts from their book: *"Rebirthing In The New Age."* Thankyou.

Therese Hollingsworth — Who encouraged me to keep writing when I nearly quit, and who typed a large part of this work. Thanks Therese.

Karin Schouten — Who also typed a large part of this work and graciously put up with my constant spelling mistakes and difficulty in reading my handwriting. Thanks Karin.

Frank and William Gunn — Who greatly supported my work and helped in the promotion of this book. Thankyou both.

Kathryn Richardson — who was my constant companion, support and chief inspirator throughout the latter, and most important time of my writings. Thanks Kathryn.

Gerry Atkinson — Who did the final proof reading and editing and greatly supported the promotion of this book. Thanks so much Gerry.

Darag and Margaret Rennie — Who contributed to my experience as a seminar leader and training as a Rebirther. Thanks.

William Heinemann Ltd. — Thankyou for your kind permission to use extracts from "The Prophet" by Kahlil Gibran.

Alan Grantham — Who contributed to my training as a Rebirther. Thanks Alan.

John Wolfe — Who first introduced me to Rebirthing. Thankyou John.

Frances Andrijich — Photographer for the cover. An excellent job. Thanks Frances.

Judy Niemiec — Graphic designer for the cover. A wonderful job, second to none. Thanks Judy.

To the inspirational writings of other authors who inspired and assisted in the creation of this work: Dr Wayne Dyer, Michael Freedman, Vernon Howard, Kyle King, Ken Keyes, Jim Leonard, Phil Laut, Jim Morningstar. Thankyou.

Daphne, Dora and Dead-eyed Dick — Great inspiration through their sillyness and fun. Thanks Guys.

Peter Quinn — Who designed the Logo. Thanks Peter.

To all my Rebirthing clients who contributed in some way to my knowledge and experience in Rebirthing during the two years of writing this work (1982—1984). Thankyou all most sincerely.

FOREWORD

I dedicate this work to YOU; all you beautiful people who have the courage to make those changes in your lives that will enable you to find your own true Selves.

REBIRTHING
(Conscious Connected Breathing)

Correct breathing is the most basic form of healing.

A person can go for three months without food; three days without water, but only three minutes without air.

'Then the Lord God took some soil from the ground and formed a man out of it; he breathed into his nostrils the breath of life, and man became a living Being'. (Genesis 2:7)

My purpose in writing this book is to present another approach to Rebirthing as a result of my personal experience, as well as to offer a number of techniques that can help you to find your own pathway to 'Self-Realisation'. The term is used here to describe the journey into the soul and deeper consciousness, for the purpose of discovering the 'Kingdom of Heaven' within us all.

In 1983, Phil Laut and Jim Leonard wrote a wonderful book: 'Rebirthing, the Science of Enjoying All of Your Life'.

Their work is a major contribution to the Science of Rebirthing, and what I have written here will, I trust, supplement it in some way. In describing the actual technique of Rebirthing, our approach is very similar in that it aims at keeping it gentle, easy and enjoyable. Although my description of the process is very similar to Phil's and Jim's, I have focused this work mainly on the love and acceptance of life, and in the area of 'personal law', which deals with causes of unhappiness, stress and suppressed energy.

GETTING THE MOST OUT OF THIS BOOK

This book is best used in conjunction with regular Rebirthing sessions (on a once-a-week basis) in order to truly relate to each step and aspect of the process. I wrote it with this idea in mind. The following outline is how I work with my Rebirthing clients. After each session I set them certain breathing and mental exercises to do along with personal reading at home from this book.

The first 7 chapters before their first Rebirthing session.

Chapter 8 (Focusing Awareness) before their second session.

Chapters 9—10 (Bliss Conscious and Don Quixote) before their third session.

Chapters 11—12 (Relaxation and Affirmations) before their fourth session.

Chapters 13—17 (The Personal Laws) before their fifth session.

Chapters 18—21 (Self-sabotage, Conditioning and The Anatomy of Fear) before their sixth session.

Chapters 22—23 (Self-love and Acceptance) before their seventh session.

Chapters 24—26 (Forgiveness, Self-Responsibility and Self-Expression) before their eighth session.

Chapters 27—28 (Health and Water Rebirthing) before their ninth session.

Chapters 29—30 (Self- Rebirthing and Last Words) before their tenth session.

NOTE: This process can change your life. It is an exciting adventure deep into your heart, while expanding self-awareness to embrace the total environment as well.

CONTENTS

Page

Part One — The REBIRTHING Technique

Chapter 1   REBIRTHING Made Easy   3
2   Conscious Connected Breathing   13
3   Total Awareness   18
4   Total Acceptance   20
5   Total Relaxation   26
6   Whatever Happens is the Right Happening   28
7   The REBIRTHING Cycle   30
8   Focusing Awareness   34
9   Bliss Consciousness   45
10   Don Quixote   61
11   The Art of Relaxation   65
12   Affirmations — Creating Positive Reality   73

Part Two — Unravelling Our Personal Law

Chapter 13   Personal Law   87
14   The Birth Trauma   93
15   The Unconscious Death Urge   95
16   Other Life-times   100
17   Authority Disapproval Syndrome   102
18   Self-Sabotage Conditioning   106
19   The Blaming and Not-Fair Syndrome   117
20   The Tyranny of Must, Shoulds and Oughts   122
21   The Anatomy of Fear   126

Part Three — The Art of Learning, Loving and Living

Chapter 22   Self Love   133
23   Self-Acceptance   145
24   Forgiveness   160
25   Self-Responsibility   165
26   Self-Expression   175
27   General Health   180
28   Water REBIRTHING   182
29   Self-REBIRTHING   185
30   Last Words   189

About the Author   193

PART ONE

THE BREATHING TECHNIQUE

CHAPTER 1

REBIRTHING MADE EASY

WHAT IS REBIRTHING?

The science of rebirthing is a personal process, using a breathing technique to clear out physical, mental and emotional blocks or stresses, especially those arising from birth and early life experiences. The origin of most human behavioural difficulties is in very early childhood experiences. By activating past traumatic experiences suppressed in deeper consciousness and gently letting go of them, we achieve a joyful integration of energies, which enhance our capacity to enjoy life more fully, with ourselves and with others.

THE TECHNIQUE is called REBIRTHING for two reasons:

1. The process gives a person the seeming experience of a brand new start at life, with a clearer sense of purpose, greater joy, and more compassion. It is a wonderful adventure deep into your own heart, yet it expands your awareness to embrace the whole world as well.

2. The process evokes a person's natural sense of relaxation and enjoyment. It expands consciousness and therefore encompasses all past experience, and releases the trauma of them. This can sometimes involve the memories of one's own birth.

WHAT ARE SUPPRESSIONS?

Suppressions are pockets of stress and tension which are created when there is conflict in the mind. Conflict is created in the mind when we try to avoid so-called traumatic experiences, because we have perceived that experience as bad, painful or unpleasant.

In order to cope with major difficulties in our lives, our 'ego' (learned habitual conditioning) acts as a built-in safety mechanism

3

and withdraws our awareness away from the experience in order to cope and begin feeling better again. But in actual fact, nothing can ever be avoided. If we try, we only suppress that experience. That suppression acts as an energy 'block' to our natural flow of love, joy and inner peace.

Deep within the memory banks of our brain are the memories of every experience in this lifetime. The experiences that were perceived as unpleasant or traumatic have often been suppressed in order to cope with the situation at the time. But to suppress something is to hold it in check, to restrain it, to place an inhibition on it. This requires a constant stream of energy to hold the suppression of the stress in the body or the mind, which leads to fatigue, disease, and eventually death. For example, if we tense the muscles in our arm, and hold the tension there, we are burning energy. It is the same with suppressed blocks in the system. There is a constant drain of subtle energy twenty-four hours a day, seven days a week, year after year. Sleep and normal rest do not release these tensions, and most people live out their entire lives with this extra burden.

INTEGRATION

Integration is the object of rebirthing. We define 'integration' as the coming together and working in unity of the three functions: the INTELLECT, the EMOTIONS, and the PHYSICAL. When there are blocks in the system, the three functions act independently of each other, with one predominant over the others, creating disharmony. This imbalance affects every area of a person's life. When the three functions are integrated, all limitations fall away, resulting in all parts of the person supporting their aliveness, effectiveness and pleasure. This is the long-term goal of rebirthing. In the short term, we aim at clearing the suppressions, which many rebirthers also term INTEGRATION.

Most rebirthers prefer to use the term INTEGRATION rather than the term 'release', because 'release' suggests getting rid of something less than perfect. The fact is that there is never anything bad or wrong to let go of, and believing that there was, was the original cause of all suppressions.

It is all in how we perceive something. If we see something and believe it is wrong or bad, then our reaction is likely to be one of rejection and a withdrawal of our awareness. This is a form of hatred and the cause of suppression. The truth is that we experienced something that was perfect in the first place, and then we decided that it was wrong or bad. Integration is the process of allowing what we had once tried to make wrong, through our thoughts and suppression, right, by consciously being aware of a sense of freedom and perfection.

Our approach is to love all of ourselves and this includes those things we once decided to think of as bad or wrong.

SUPPRESSION AND INTEGRATION

The word suppression in the context that we are using here means to restrain, hold down, hide away and control. As integration is the objective of rebirthing, it is therefore the opposite to suppression. Anything that exists can be perceived as being enjoyed or disliked, good or bad, loved or hated. It has little to do with the thing itself, but is instead, our decision about it. By believing that something is bad or wrong, creates a duality and a separation from truth. There is nothing in existence that is bad or wrong, only our perception and how we choose to see things. For example, a family going into the country for a picnic are frustrated and angry because it began to rain and spoiled their day. But the farmers are very happy about the rain which waters their pastures and crops. This shows there is neither good nor bad, but simply different viewpoints and how people choose to see things. Believing something is wrong or bad is the same as believing that emotional feelings and physical sensations in the body are bad or wrong.

Truth is perfect. Everything is true and therefore perfect. But if we perceive something (which is perfect) and decide that it is not perfect and therefore bad, we make it wrong. Yet it is not the action or feeling that is wrong, but the thought behind it that is wrong. The only things that are 'wrong' in the universe are points of view. Our limited way of seeing things, which is always through the 'ego', is a conditioned reflex action.

Another example is, if for any reason we decided not to like apple pie; then what we are doing is deciding to have an unpleasant feeling in our physical body everytime we eat or even think about apple pie. The apple pie is the same, whether we like it or not. It just IS! If sometime we ate some apple pie and decided to enjoy it, then this would be the same as changing our decision of how good or bad it was. It works the same way in everything, including our likes in music, family fights, opposing political parties, physical pain, fear, and so on. The key is in the decision of how we respond, and not in the thing itself. A decision to love is always a decision to enjoy and feel good, and we always have that choice.

The PROCESS OF SUPPRESSION is deciding to see something as bad or unpleasant, and then in an effort to feel good, to withdraw our awareness of it.

The PROCESS OF INTEGRATION is permitting ourselves to become fully aware of something we once avoided through suppression and now choose to enjoy it.

How can we decide to love something we hate? Chapter nine 'Bliss-Consciousness', explains how.

Whenever a person has a thought, he or she creates a similar type pattern of energy in the physical body, which eventually manifests in a person's life. For example, if a person has the thought, 'people hurt me', this thought will cause fear in his body and negative reactions from people in his life. If he suppresses the fear he experiences, the thought will become an unquestioned reality. The fear will become unconscious tension and the negative reactions from people will reinforce his negative belief, causing him to withdraw further and further away from people and life. But he could change this pattern at any time simply by choosing to do so, or, by getting rebirthed and integrating the fear.

When a suppression occurs through fear or whatever, a person also suppresses the negative thought behind the belief about the experience. When an idea or belief is suppressed, it lodges in the subconscious and is no longer a mere belief, but is experienced as that person's reality. The 'hard realities' and struggles that some people claim life is all about, are expressing the way they view life and shows the extent of their suppressed negative beliefs and experiences that person has. It's like looking out of a wet window while it is raining, with the glass giving the impression of a distorted and blurred world, and believing it to be reality.

We can also describe suppression in terms of the relationship between the physical body and the 'Life Force' within us. The 'Life Force' is a form of consciousness which is best described as SELF AWARENESS, or higher consciousness.

Self-awareness is the ability to be consious of the three functions, the Intellect, the Emotions, and the Physical body, as well as the exterior world at the same time. This feat of consciousness is beyond the scope of most people because few are fully integrated and thus fail to experience such a phenomenon. Higher consciousness is also an awareness beyond our three functional self and has been described as a 'transcendental' state which can be experienced in deep meditation and often in rebirthing. This is a process by which consciousness is expanded as the result of the system becoming clearer of energy blocks. As the natural flow of energy increases, the 'Life Force' vitalises and invigorates our total being.

Conscious awareness is the energising focal-point of the 'Life Force' and suppression is the withdrawal of awareness from parts of the physical body over a long period in order to avoid some experience.

So, to withdraw the awareness away from an unpleasant experience, is to actually withdraw the life force from part of our physical body. The 'unpleasant' pattern of energy having nowhere to go as a result of not being integrated, lodges in the muscles and manifests itself as stress or tension, and remains in the physical body even though we are not aware of it. The sickest people are those who have a lot of tension but feel nothing.

The 'Life Force' is the organising mechanism of molecules that take the form of the physical body. When we withdraw our awareness from any part of the physical body because we think something is unpleasant, we cause an interruption of the life-giving energy flow to that area of the body. As a result, the molecules become less organised and ageing and disease occur. The interrupted energy blocks eventually influence the rest of the body, causing more blocks, resulting in an overall condition of less sensitivity, less awareness, less aliveness, and more suppression. In this way, once suppression has begun, it usually creates a build-up of layers of stress and a further gradual lessening of the Life Force to the whole physical body. Death occurs as a total suppression of the organism. It seems that most people begin the process of suppressing at birth. If you cannot remember your birth, then you probably began suppressing at that point.

ACTIVATION is a term that refers to becoming aware of suppressed energy patterns; the 'made wrongs' of the past. Yet, it is not important to regress to the original experience where we made it wrong by avoiding it; or even remember it. Occasionally, memories of the past will occur when a suppression surfaces through activation, but mostly they don't. Memories are not important. What is significant is the activated energy patterns moving through the body and mind and being totally aware of these. This awareness expands the conscious mind and speeds up the process of integration.

It is easier to integrate every experience than to suppress them. For example, if we hold a pen tightly in our hand, we are burning energy. All that is necessary to let go of the pen, is to stop flexing the muscles in the hand and the pen will drop away. All that is necessary to integrate anything is to stop 'making it wrong'. This goes for everything in our lives. It is easier to succeed in life than to fail. It is easier to be happy than to be unhappy. It is easier to love than to hate. We don't have to do anything to live, love and have fun. But we do have to do something not to enjoy life, and that is in the blocking off of ourselves from our natural Life Force and the flow of the Truth in each of us. Therefore, in theory, it is so easy to integrate anything, once it is activated. In practical terms, however, it is not so easy. Why? Because we are masters of suppression and we have probably been practicing making perfect situations wrong for a long time, and the habit of suppressing and seeing experiences as bad could be well entrenched.

The difficulty lies in deep ingrained conditioned habits. We are so mechanical because we are controlled by our conditioned 'brain-washed' subconscious minds. It is the subconscious which we don't experience because it is in a state of suppression and that is why it is subconscious and unconscious. However, we discuss this in detail in chapter 9.

SOCIETY IS BASED ON SUPPRESSION

We have all suppressed something at sometime. We have a pain and we go to the Doctor who gives us a pill to relieve the symptom, which suppresses it. (Rebirthing is about treating causes and not just symptoms.) We take aspirins for fever, which suppresses it.

On a psychological level we hang on to our suppressions and tensions because we are not aware of them as such. But we do feel anxious, fearful, resentful, sad, lonely, etc. at times, and we blame these feelings on other people. The emotions we feel are due to our resisting the fact that everything is perfect in the first place.

We hang on to our suppressions because our ego thinks that to let go means losing a part of ourselves. So we identify ourselves with our feelings, thinking they are us, instead of only belonging to us. Therefore, we keep them suppressed and stuffed down to hide them out of the way. However, we can only hold so many suppressions before the body and mind react and refuse to hold any more. So, negative emotions, like fear, anger, sadness etc. begin to surface at the least provocation. We are easily triggered off by other peoples' activated suppressions, and our emotions feed off someone elses, creating disharmony and conflict between them and us. At such times we need help to keep our suppressions locked away so they won't

8

bother us. To do this we call on the aid of drugs, to help us suppress disturbing emotional feelings, highly distressing mental activity and even physical pain.

Anaethesia, as administered by hospitals and dentists, is all about suppressing physical pain. Tranquilisers work on calming the mind,as well as muscles, by suppressing their function. Sleeping pills and tranquilisers are so widely used they reveal the overwhelming problem of suppression in our society. Prescription drugs like valium, and recreational drugs like alcohol, nicotine, caffeine, marijuana, etc. work at suppressing emotions. For instance, although some people can respond differently, generally alcohol suppresses the emotion of fear. When a person experiences fear, the blood vessels shrink causing the face to go white. Alcohol swells the blood vessels, making the person feel better temporarily. Observe any heavy drinker and you will see someone who prefers to drink themselves to death, rather than express their fear.

Generally, nicotine suppresses anger. The reaction of anger makes the blood vessels expand, which causes a person to go red in the face, yet nicotine suppresses this emotion on a physical level by causing the blood vessels to shrink

Caffeine addiction is common through the consumption of coffee and generally suppresses the results of anaesthesia as well as other forms of suppression. Because of the high consumption of energy needed to hold down suppressions, very suppressed people probably feel the need to have regular doses of caffeine simply to sustain their familiar level of suppression, which feels comfortable.

Marijuana generally suppresses sadness. Psychedelic drugs like LSD, etc. mainly work as 'super-stimulants' and the reason people experience what is normally an unfamiliar personal response is that drugs like LSD suppress the suppression. Stimulants are the most widely used and the most suppressive drugs of all, and can generally suppress just about anything. But stimulants often create an addiction and a dependency, and anything that creates such a demanding addiction is a form of suppression operating in the system. It has been found that the considerable use of stimulants over a long period of time results in the deterioration of the mind as well as the physical body. Drugs have a suppressing effect, and anything that destroys the body or mind is a form of suppression of one kind or another.

If any of the above substances are part of your life, try giving them up completely for a month, and this will tell you whether or not you are using them to suppress anything. Any form of addiction is suppressive, and it could include any habitual distraction — watching T.V., overeating, sleeping, jogging, constantly talking, having parties and so on. You can add your own addictive activities that distract you from your feelings.

The person who indulges in the odd glass of wine, smokes a cigar at Christmas, or even smokes a 'joint' of marijuana now and again, cannot be regarded as using any of them as a form of suppression. What is being said is that in using the above chemicals or activities habitually to hold down and avoid our feelings, is a suppressant of one kind or another.

THE BIRTH TRAUMA

At the moment we were born, we formed impressions about the world, which were either positive or negative. If it was a traumatic birth, such as the clatter of pans, blinding lights, loud voices, and the cutting of the umbilical cord before we were breathing on our own, (as is the case in many hospitals), then there is a good chance that we adopted a negative impression about this new environment we had entered. This is the beginning of 'the world is against me' syndrome, which we have carried ever since. These impressions control us from a subconscious level and influence every area of our lives.

Just because we were unable to verbalise our thoughts when we were a baby doesn't mean we were unable to feel and be capable of some sophisticated deductions about that supposedly traumatic event. In fact, at birth we were more aware of what was happening to us than anytime since. Some of the generalisations we may have made at birth could have included:

● Life is a struggle.
● The universe is hostile and against me.
● People hurt me.
● I am not wanted.
● There must be something wrong with me.
● I can't get enough (air, love, etc.)

As a newborn, nature provides that we receive oxygen through the umbilical cord while learning to breathe in our new environment (having been in fluid for so long), but the custom has been to cut the cord immediately, throwing us into a panic where it felt like we would die right there at birth. Thus, we most likely took a deep breath, and the air hitting our delicate lungs for the first time produced excruciating pain. Breathing became associated with pain, and our breathing has been too shallow ever since.

Then we were probably separated from our mother, covered with a fabric too rough for our delicate skin and placed in a little box in the nursery. This mishandling and, in particular, the separation of mother and child is so traumatic that most of us never recover from this devastating experience.

Fortunately, there are some changes being made since Doctor Frederic Le Boyer, a French obstetrician, began delivering babies in a trauma-free atmosphere, making it a pleasure to be born.

At the time Doctor Le Boyer was developing his process in France, Leonard Orr in California was developing Rebirthing and helping people of all ages to get in touch with their birth trauma and integrate it.

During Rebirthing sessions, the object is to integrate material as soon as possible, adding comfort and enjoyment for the rebirthee. Integration can take place even when each pattern of energy is still at a very subtle level of awareness. Irrespective of how dramatic or frightening some experience was when it was suppressed, it can be easily Integrated during a session while still very subtle. If Integration doesn't happen when the activated energy is subtle, it gradually becomes more and more intense, until the Rebirthee is finally forced through exhaustion to surrender to it. At this point the energy will either become enjoyable or vanish. The term 'surrender' means dropping our defences, ceasing the struggle that is necessary to keep suppressed material out of our awareness, and extending acceptance to all parts of our being.

So the technique involves expanding awareness of suppressed material and surrendering to it. 'Forced' surrender, because of the intensity due to one's resistance, achieves results but is not as enjoyable. A rebirthee who learns to integrate activated material at a subtle level will have a much greater sense of safety with the process, which results in keeping it gentle and a willingness to allow the suppressions to surface with ease and enjoyment.

Rebirthing is easy to learn. The results are permanent, and about 95% of it is intensely pleasurable. The 5% of rebirthing that is not enjoyable is due to people's unwillingness to give up their familiar inner suffering. All discomfort in the process is due to not letting go and surrendering negativity, stress and pain. This is not surprising when it's considered that a person who has habitually carried a negative trait or a suppressed tension for years may not be ready to give up something which is familiar, even though painful, for the experience of being without it. The change may be too much to take. But others, willing not to obstruct their own growth by 'unlearning' and integrating the suppressed negativities, can make the experience of moving energy highly pleasurable. The energy that moves in the body and mind during rebirthing is a person's own pure 'Life Force' cleaning the dust from the system.

Rebirthing can be best described as the process by which we eliminate mental and emotional 'junk' held in the physical body. The technique is so simple that it can be practiced by anyone. The word 'junk' refers to energy that is no longer needed, and not something that is bad. While learning the process it is necessary to work with a Rebirther who has learned to enjoy his or her own energy. A 'beginner' can feel safe with them.

Rebirthing works best when it is gentle and pleasant, and the Rebirther's role is to ensure this outcome. Some people think rebirthing is about confronting suppressions and some people do rebirth this way, yet that is not what we are involved with. Our aim is to make the whole process informative, pleasant and relaxing.

For this reason, even though rebirthing is a single process, there has been added an additional four components to be incorporated with the breathing, which gives greater efficiency and more enjoyment. So, rebirthing is a single process involving five components.

THE FIVE COMPONENTS OF REBIRTHING

1. Conscious Connected Breathing.
2. Total Awareness.
3. Total Acceptance.
4. Total Relaxation.
5. Whatever happens is the Right Happening.

Each component will be explained in detail.

CHAPTER 2

THE FIRST COMPONENT:
CONSCIOUS CONNECTED BREATHING

The breath is the link between the Life-force and the physical body, and by consciously connecting our breath, we bring all parts of the body to our awareness. Suppressed material becomes 'activated', which means it begins to come up to the surface level of consciousness.

Basically, we connect the inner breath, the Life-Force or 'Prana', with the outer breath of the respiratory system. We consciously reconnect all parts of our being, expanding our awareness of self, others, the universe, Truth, and radiating compassion.

When a person suppresses something, the breath is very much affected in as much as it becomes controlled on the exhale, and even held for a time. When a person is emotionally upset, particularly with fear, their breath becomes laboured and controlled. This is when suppression is taking place and so inhibited breathing and suppression are one and the same process.

On the mental level, we suppress things by withdrawing our awareness away from the experience. On the physical level, we suppress our breathing in order to facilitate the action of suppression. That is why we use a breathing technique to activate or loosen the suppressions. As inhibited breathing is the physical act of suppressing, we use full relaxed breathing as a means of reversing the process, bringing us back into balance, and breathing freely, fully and uncontrolled.

So Conscious Connected Breathing is exactly opposite to the type of breathing that is used to suppress and hold the suppressions in the subconscious. When our breathing is consciously connected, the energy that is needed to hold down the suppression is removed, and the suppressions begin surfacing to our conscious level of mind.

CONSCIOUS CONNECTED BREATHING involves the following two points:

1. The INHALE is connected to the EXHALE with no pause in between.
2. The EXHALE is TOTALLY RELAXED and not controlled in any way.

It is helpful to breath through either the mouth or the nose as this helps keep the inhale and the exhale connected, rather than in through one and out through the other.

We simply pull in the inhale and completely relax the exhale. We don't force the exhale, nor do we control it in any way whatsoever; we let gravity expell it for us.

THE BREATH RELEASE relates to a complete uninhibited breathing, which includes a total letting go, even collapsing on the exhale. When we suppress something, the body puts a new inhibition into the breathing mechanism in order to keep the energy suppressed. It's like partly turning off a water tap, interrupting the natural flow. Different instances of suppression puts blocks in different areas of the lungs, chest, abdominal and shoulder muscles, the trachea, sinuses, nose and mouth, which not only burn up energy for no good reason, but inhibit the vital nourishment of oxygen through 'under breathing'.

Whenever some material is integrated, the breathing mechanism becomes more free. The classical BREATH-RELEASE happens when we integrate the trauma of our first breath, and it is occasionally accompanied with choking and gasping for air, followed by a great opening and relaxing of the breath. But in most cases the BREATH-RELEASE is accomplished when we are using connected breathing, completely uninhibited, without necessarily any choking.

Various Types of Conscious Connected Breathing:

1. FULL and SLOW. This is when we take in more air than we would normally do while resting. FULL and SLOW is the most widely used breathing method in a session because it sends the maximum of energy throughout the body, loosening suppressed material. It's most effective at the beginning of a session or after Integration and rest, when you are ready to start on the next cycle.
2. FAST and SHALLOW. This is breathing in and out very fast, and is similar to an old steam engine going up a hill. FAST and SHALLOW is the most effective when the material that is coming up is very intense. The increased speed of the breathing leads to Integration and the

shallowness lessens the intensity of the pattern. It is helpful when using this type of breathing to stay focussed on the pattern of energy and exactly where in the body it is happening.

3. FAST and FULL. We will sometimes be instructed by our rebirther to breathe FAST and FULL when we begin to lose consciousness by going to sleep. The increased breathing brings our awareness back into the body, leading to Integration.

Through this technique we endeavour to become fully conscious of the present moment, which helps us become aware of two things:

(i)   An awareness of the entire experience, and,

(ii) to focus our attention on the main pattern of energy coming up. Breathing fast increases the awareness of the overall experience, and breathing slow increases the focus. So, by breathing slow we maximise our focus to become fully conscious of our activated suppressed material. As we become totally aware of the energy and then speed up the breathing we expand our overall awareness leading to Integration.

An important point here is that we are discussing the speed and volume of the inhale and not the exhale. We should never control the exhale in any way whatsoever. It does not matter if the exhale is faster or slower than the inhale, or of the same duration. Let the body decide and completely relax the exhale.

With regards to the three types of connected breathing already mentioned, we each find our own breathing rhythms in time. Generally, with experience and increased confidence in the process, our breathing will tend to adjust itself to what is happening in the rest of our body quite naturally.

BREATHING THROUGH THE NOSE OR MOUTH

Whether we breathe through the nose or the mouth, depends on personal preference. However, at times of intense activation it can be more effective to breathe through the mouth to increase the air intake.

BREATHING INTO THE UPPER OR LOWER PART OF THE LUNGS?

Generally, if energy is being activated in the lower part of the body from the waist down it can be helpful to breathe in the lower part of the lungs. If energy is activated in the upper part of the body such as head, chest, or arms, it can be helpful to breathe into the upper part of the lungs. However, the reverse is sometimes true. It can happen that a pattern of energy in the upper part of the body has its parallel breathing restriction in the lower part of the lungs or vice-versa. By observing our avoidance of breathing in a certain part of the lungs and then by directing the breath there, can often cause activation of suppressed material from that area. **Important point.**

TETANY

Tetany is a term which refers to the involuntary temporary paralysis of certain muscles that can sometimes happen during a session. When it happens, it does so mostly in the hands and facial muscles, particularly around the mouth, but it can happen anywhere in the body. There is nothing harmful or wrong about tetany during Rebirthing, or even uncomfortable, unless one resists and struggles against it. Almost everyone who has been rebirthed has experienced it. The cause of tetany is in our controlling the exhale in some way. Either holding onto the exhale, or forcing the exhale can cause it. Tetany can be eliminated by understanding that there is nothing to resist that is bad, and by relaxing the exhale and relaxing in general. If it comes up intensely, then focus on the sensation and go with it. Breathe fast and shallow and it will integrate rapidly. Above all, avoid thinking that tetany is wrong, bad, and even unpleasant. It is perfectly OK to experience it, and with more experience the likelihood of tetany is lessened.

HYPERVENTILATION

Hyperventilation is described as a dramatic loss of carbon dioxide in the blood as a result of very deep breathing. The symptoms are experienced as dizziness, or breathlessness, and feelings of panic. Hyperventilation is only possible when the breath is inhibited in some way, and therefore is not necessary to the Rebirthing process. It is really caused by forcing or 'blowing' the exhale. People who are afraid of their feelings and their thoughts, start to push on the exhale when suppressed material starts to come up. They begin to push on the exhale as if they were ridding the body of something bad. The less relaxed a person is about the Rebirthing process, the more likely he or she is to experience the inconvenience of hyperventilation. A way to treat hyperventilation is to breathe into a container like a paper bag, or even your cupped hands so that the air you breathe has a high proportion of carbon dioxide. The symptoms would pass, but only temporarily, for you are likely to start forcing the exhale again if the cause is not removed. If the exhale is completely uninhibited and relaxed, hyperventilation can not happen, even when the fastest and fullest breathing is used.

If Rebirthing was only the breathing technique (as it was when it was first discovered), the process would still work but a person would have to do conscious connected breathing for quite some time before achieving integration. Besides, it probably wouldn't be very comfortable either. The breathing which activates the suppressed material does not cause the actual integration. It is through the other four components of Rebirthing, which not only cause integration, but also make the whole process highly pleasurable. So with only conscious connected breathing, the activated material would be almost as unpleasant as when it was first suppressed.

In Rebirthing with just relaxing on the exhale and keeping the breath connected is often enough to complete the breathing cycle. However, if a person is unconsciously committed to their pain and struggle, the fear of the suppressed material can increase making the experience more intense and traumatic. This can continue until finally out of sheer exhaustion of holding suppressed patterns at such a gross level of consciousness, they would be forced to surrender and Integrate it. It's rather like trying to hold down an inflatable rubber boat that is inflating beneath the water.

Using the other four components of Rebirthing, we are able to relax and 'surrender' right from the beginning, making it highly enjoyable and far more effective.

Up to now we have laid special emphasis on the exhale and keeping it relaxed. It has been found in our experience that this is best achieved by keeping the inhale fairly gentle and not trying too hard.

CHAPTER 3

THE SECOND COMPONENT:
TOTAL AWARENESS

Total awareness in Rebirthing refers to being acutely aware of what is taking place within the body. This is done by focusing on feelings and sensations that come to our attention as the result of activated energy patterns. This greatly aids the 're-connection' of our Lifeforce, or consciousness with our physical body, activating suppressed energy patterns.

'Energy patterns' refers to any thought, feeling or sensation we experience in the present moment. It can range from tingling in our fingers, being aware of dogs barking next door, intense energy in various parts of the body, in fact a whole range of emotional feelings. This could extend to even a full or partial memory recall of some event early in life.

So we define energy patterns as any experience that is part of our subjective reality in the present moment. Being aware of these details expands our consciousness, broadens our universe, and extends our Lifeforce. It is simply focusing our full attention or awareness on what is happening at the time.

In Rebirthing, total awareness means that we are fully aware of the PRESENT MOMENT. The present moment is perfect bliss. It is impossible to suffer or be unhappy in the present moment. Consider this. The next time you are feeling unhappy, look closely and you will see how it is linked to something that has already happened in the past, or something you think will happen in the future. If you are unhappy with a present existing situation, it is because you are comparing it with a memory of a more pleasant past experience, or with a hopeful expectation of the future.

If we get nothing more out of Rebirthing than learning how to focus our awareness on to what is happening in our bodies and minds, we will have learned a technique so valuable, that it alone can take us all the way to 'Self-Realisation'.

Total awareness not only speeds up the activating of suppressed energy patterns, but also accelerates integration, making the second component a vital part of the overall process of Rebirthing.

CHAPTER 4

THE THIRD COMPONENT:
TOTAL ACCEPTANCE (BLISS CONSCIOUSNESS)

Total acceptance in Rebirthing refers to accepting and loving the energy that moves within the body during a Rebirthing session. This energy can manifest itself as an intense emotion like sadness, anger, fear, etc.; to physical sensations ranging from tingling to more intense energy patterns. Initially, our old conditioning may try to tell us that this energy is unpleasant or uncomfortable, but this is the same conditioning that had us suppressing things in the first place. So we need to make some changes in our attitude towards how we view things, which will assist us in making Rebirthing one of the most enjoyable experiences of our lifetime.

To do this, let us consider a simple yet dynamic idea, which I regard as the basic philosophy behind Rebirthing.

"We are all in a perfect state of Bliss, whether we are aware of it or not."

To take this further, all life forms, all situations, all conditions are in a state of perfection. This being the case (which is explained in depth in Chapter 9, Bliss-Consciousness), we each stand as we are in a state of Bliss, but most of us are quite unaware of it.

This means that even though a person's 'inner true self' experiences everything in a state of perfect bliss, the mind does not always perceive things in this way. This is because the mind has become conditioned into believing that certain things are bad, unpleasant, evil or wrong. Although our Inner True Self experiences everything ecstatically, the surface conditioned mind distorts the truth and makes what a person perceives appear as an illusion. Thus, the surface conscious mind is denied the experience of Bliss, and Rebirthing is about bringing Bliss up to the surface mind where we can enjoy it consciously.

Bliss consciousness is not just an emotion. It is a state of Perfect Being, of 'pure existing' in the ever present moment.

Bliss consciousness could be defined as being conscious of the highest good within us; that perfect spark of the Divine. Jesus* (Yehoshuwah Ben-Miriam) explained it as the 'Kingdom of Heaven within'; Buddhists call it 'Nirvana'; Gurdjieff† termed it 'Objective Consciousness'.

Basically it is the ability to stand back from our function and observe the true reality within. Our function being our expression which is our mind and body and not our True Self. We must remember that WE are not our function. We are TRUTH.

We know that we are not our mind or body, because we are - *experiencing* our mind and body, and we cannot be what we see or experience, anymore than the eyes can see themselves. An Experiencer is quite different and apart from any experience.

For an Experiencer to exist, He has to have an object of experience, which is separate from Him.

This becomes clearer when we understand that the present moment is all that exists. Nothing real exists outside of the present moment. Memories of yesterday and imaginings of tomorrow are just thought forms in the mind with little relevance to the here and now.

Awareness is what we are. We are not the ego, the mind, the personality, or even the body. We are not the container of awareness, which most of us identify ourselves with, but instead we are consciousness Itself. We are not one who is aware; We are the Awareness.

Our mind and body is the experience, but as Awareness, We are the Experiencer. As the Experiencer We experience each new second as it arrives Blissfully, for We are incapable of experiencing time any other way. It is the mind which changes reality into illusion by comparing our present situation with that of a past situation, or even a hopeful future, and not living in the present moment. When the mind compares one experience with another, it denies the reality of the present moment and thus perceives frustration, fear, loneliness,

---

*Yehoshuwah Ben-Miriam was Jesus' real name. It was changed to Jesus when the Bible was translated into Greek — Jesus is a Greek name.
†George Ivanovitch Gurdjieff, (Approx 1872—1949) a Russian, a great teacher of Esoteric Truths, established his 'school' in Paris in the early 1920's. G.I. Gurdjieff has had a profound influence upon my life and it is reflected throughout most of my writings.

suffering, etc.

When we are not in the present moment, our True Self (the Experiencer) goes to sleep. Most people spend 99% of their entire lives in this state of unconsciousness. We need to wake from our dream-like state of imaginings to the reality of the present moment.

To go beyond the sphere of separation and find Oneness with the Universe, one must transcend experience to finally arrive at the transcendental' nature of pure Absolute existence. We are not the mind or the body. These are tools we use (or misuse) for the purpose of creation. They are an extension of the True Self, as a hammer is an extension of the carpenter's hand.

We are the pure Experiencer, standing apart from anything we are experiencing. Therefore, I, the soul, the Experiencer, am always in a state of sheer bliss, regardless of whatever my mind or body is experiencing. At this level, there is no judgement of right or wrong, good or bad, like or dislike, and so on. Everything just IS. Also, there is no time. There is ME and the experience of MY mind creating these experiences. So either I'm enjoying what I'm experiencing, or I'm enjoying the choice of not enjoying the experience. This is one of the secrets of Eternal happiness. Ponder this.

In a Rebirthing session, no matter what comes up, and regardless of how our mind perceived something at the time we originally suppressed it, we are Blissfully enjoying it at one level or another.

Awareness is Bliss. Life becomes fun when we bring Bliss up to our conscious level of awareness and make positive choices about any experience. When Bliss is kept at the subconscious level of awareness and we choose to hate something, dis-own it, ignore it, suppress it (which is a death urge), we suffer from it. All suffering is caused by choosing to suffer.

The key word in the last sentence is 'choosing'. We all have the choice, although most of us seem to be ignorant of this fact. It is interesting to note that the word 'ignorance' comes from the word 'ignore'. 'Ignoring' is what suppression is all about. But when we choose to give everything in our experience, total loving acceptance, take full responsibility for it, own it, love it, and love ourselves for the whole experience (which is the life urge), then suffering is impossible.

We must realise that our thoughts are the only source of everything in our personal reality, and it is important to understand that everything we experience is the satisfaction of a desire. The part of us that desired the result we are now getting, is in a state of perfect fulfillment. So, let us celebrate everything in our experience. Let us be enthusiastic about everything. If we are angry, really get into our anger. If we are afraid, really get into our fear. If we are sad, let us get enthusiastically sad, and so on.

Enthusiasm is something everyone has an unlimited supply of and it is our main motivating force. We can mop a floor, clean a room, or do any job more efficiently, if we do it enthusiastically. Enthusiasm for improvement must include acceptance for where we are now. Acceptance of our 'weaknesses' paves the way for growth that is 'fun'. Making a feeling wrong (or anything else for that matter), means using a part of our energy to suppress the uncomfortable feelings. Feelings just are, and can never be wrong. Those negative emotions are just our resistance against truth when we are not in the present moment. By being truthful to the present moment, we are able to surrender to any emotion, enjoy it and therefore integrate it.

Pain is a word invented by confused people who see energy as something that is bad, hurtful and unpleasant. Pain does not exist except in the mind. Energy exists, and at times it can get pretty intense. The only difference between energy and pain is that a person can enjoy their energy while the person who feels pain suffers from it.

Feeling energy is important to us because when we feel intense energy somewhere in the body, it is a message that something needs our attention, some organ is unbalanced or under stress, or is becoming diseased. If we cut ourselves, the energy we feel is telling us that we need to stop the flow of blood, and perhaps cover the wound.

There is no suggestion here that we suppress our pain, but rather change our point of view. Instead of feeling our energy as pain, we feel it simply as energy. We change our reference point and how we perceive our energy. Thus we need to change our conditioning, which tells us (and has probably done so since our first breath) that certain energy is painful or unpleasant. Thus, we will always suffer from pain, for the word 'pain' is part of our conditioning. If we are conditioned to believe that energy is pain, then everytime we feel intense energy we will suffer. So by changing our point of view from pain to energy, we begin to conquer pain and begin to enjoy our energy.

When Jesus was nailed to the cross, no doubt he felt the energy intensely, probably more so that we would with his highly evolved sense of awareness, but he didn't suffer from it. Jesus, who was self-realised and experienced bliss-consciousness, could look into the eyes of his torturers with complete compassion, for he understood where they were at and why they were doing it. He could love his own energy as well as those around him at the same time, because there was no hate in him, only love. It is love that is the secret of mastering the Bliss-Consciousness principle. It is love and only love that will save us from our conditioning. It is love that will save the world and love comes from total acceptance.

The study of perception is an interesting one. The Truth tells us that there is absolutely nothing in the universe that is bad, evil, painful or unpleasant; in fact the universe is here to love and support us. That is Truth. It is only our perception of mind that tells us unpleasant things exist. As our perception, that is, the way we perceive or view things, is totally controlled by our conditioned mind, our perception is distorted into seeing things the way our conditioning demands. I found this by the following experiment.

By placing one hand in warm water and the other in freezing cold water for 20 minutes, I found the warm water pleasant and the cold water unpleasant. In truth, the nerve endings were sending messages to the brain, one saying hot, the other cold; that is all. But as a conditioned being, my experience of one was pleasant and the other unpleasant, instead of just hot and cold. The physical body has a wonderful ability to adjust and adapt to different temperatures. However, if two people entered a frozen stream with differently conditioned minds, the first one perceiving it as invigorating and enjoying the experience, while the other perceived it as unpleasant, could it be that the second person would eventually freeze to death?

The next question to be asked with regards to perception, is whether memory is a part of our conditiioning, or whether conditioning is a part of memory. I suggest that they are two quite different things. A person living in the present moment is no longer controlled by their conditioning because they respond to everything happening at that moment. Yet they still have their memory which they can work from. They can still tell the time, remember a person's name, but are not controlled by their memory. A conditioned person is controlled by their memory, which has become misused as a conditioning. For example, a self-realised person could see a poisonous spider and remember that it is poisonous, but respect the integrity of the spider as it is. Another person could see the same spider and hate it for being poisonous because his conditioned memory perceives a threat that must be destroyed.

When perceiving pain, or what we normally regard as unpleasant experiences, we can choose to suffer while subconsciously it is ecstasy, or we can bring that Bliss up to the conscious level by focusing our awareness and choosing to accept and love it.

Bliss is the only thing that exists, and this manifests itself as multiple forms of energy. If our mind is conditioned into believing that some experiences are unpleasant, then our conscious mind is being untruthful. To support suppression, the mind needs to create a system of falseness and lies, to maintain the original lie. The lies we tell others are nothing compared to the lies we tell ourselves. But through Rebirthing we see that the experience was really pleasurable. Therefore, the only suppression in our bodies is suppressed happiness.

Total acceptance simply means loving everything in our experience. The alternative is to hate and suppress our energy, which leads to pain and suffering. We can do absolutely nothing to change what has happened in the past, or even five seconds ago, but we can change how we respond to any situation if we are aware enough of our conditioned reactions.

By liking this and disliking that, we only end up dividing us against ourselves. But, by being aware of the present moment, we are able to accept and love every aspect of it.

CHAPTER 5

THE FOURTH COMPONENT:
TOTAL RELAXATION

Scientific studies of stress management methods have shown that to eliminate stress from the physical body, the person has to reach a state of deep relaxation. The results of Rebirthing often relaxes people more deeply than they can ever remember. In Rebirthing, where the breathing activates the suppressions, it is the ability to let go and relax which causes the actual integration. That is why the importance of 'surrender' was mentioned earlier. 'Surrender' implies giving up, letting go, no control, being taken over, and so on. But it also means not losing one's power over oneself, in fact it leads to greater power. In the context that is being used here, the word 'surrender' means total relaxation. At any time during total relaxation, the person can re-take control, so there is nothing to fear about the concept of 'surrender'.

Total relaxation is not something we do, but rather, something we don't do. It is a letting go. Or as some religious folk say, 'let go, let God'. The Rebirthing process is a complete merging into the experience which is completely harmless and safe, while the gentle energies of the life-force within us cleanse and purify the whole system.

The need to express an activated energy pattern, whether it be wanting to squirm around; to expressing an intense emotion such as screaming or crying, and so on, which can sometimes accompany an activation, is all right, and most certainly not to be avoided if it comes up spontaneously. However, such 'drama' does not cause integration and can often be used as a distraction from really feeling what is happening in the body which can delay integration and make it all so unnecessarily difficult. Some people believe that expressing emotions is the opposite to suppressing them, but this is not necessarily so. For instance, a person with a lot of suppressed anger will not clear it out by expressing his old hostility on everyone around him. Certainly, he may relieve the pressure on the surface, but no long term benefit will be achieved. In fact his hostility may become worse as he perpetuates the cycle of anger and creates a habit pattern of resentment and short temperedness. Rather, it would be more effective if he took responsibility for it and integrated it through rebirthing or some other centering type technique. For an example, in a difficult situation like being confronted by someone abusing or criticising us, we can either:

1. Express — how we feel and satisfy our desire to hurt someone, which never integrates that energy.

2. Suppress — how we feel and try to avoid feeling bad, which neither satisfies our desire to get back at someone, nor does it integrate that energy.

3. Integrate — which leads to perfect freedom. We don't have to satisfy our desires in order to integrate them. If we did have to, then every time we felt angry with someone, we would need to hurt them, even kill them, in order to satisfy our cravings. No, we need only integrate our desires for they are just another feeling and energy pattern.

In Rebirthing, expressing an emotion can be a very good way to focus in on an energy pattern. But it can also be the distraction needed to keep it suppressed, such as with sadness, fear and especially with anger.

POSITION FOR REBIRTHING

There are no fixed rules about positions, but generally it's helpful to expose one's vulnerability by lying on one's back, legs straight and arms at the sides. It's effective to become aware of the need to scratch and fidget without satisfying such needs. This can get us in touch with important energy patterns, as such distractions can keep suppressed patterns from our awareness.

When integrating intense fear or sadness it can often be helpful to curl up into a little ball like the foetal position. Possibly lying on our front can help integrate other forms of energy. The position adopted by each Rebirthee should be what feels right at the time. However, once in a particular position, remain there without moving very much otherwise continued movement can be an avoidance technique for what is coming up which reduces the efficiency of the process.

CHAPTER 6

THE FIFTH COMPONENT: WHATEVER HAPPENS IS THE RIGHT HAPPENING

Whatever happens is the right happening refers to everything being perfect in the present moment. Therefore, we don't need to *try* to integrate anything; we don't need to *try* to achieve results; we don't even need to try to Rebirth. Trying to achieve some particular result, trying to get somewhere signifies that we are not accepting our here and now experience.

It has been stated that Rebirthing is a natural healing process that anyone can do. The technique is so simple and natural that it is very difficult to do it wrong. In fact, the way to make it harder is to *try* to do it right.

Unless a person has had some experience in some form of centering type exercise of the mind like meditation, yoga, martial arts, and so on, few realise how much effort they put into doing things. Within this fifth component of Rebirthing, a person is likely to lie there *trying* to integrate material, instead of actually integrating it. The idea is to relax *trying* to integrate. It eliminates the 'musts', 'shoulds', and 'oughts' from the other four components.

All we need to do is just breathe, focus awareness, love everything and just relax and let integration happen.

When we talk about integration, it appears that we are doing something specific, but in actual fact, we have stopped making something wrong, ceased to ignore or avoid something. Instead, we have surrendered into accepting that a situation is perfect, in spite of the fact that we may have once believed that it wasn't. If something hasn't integrated, then we need only accept that it is as yet not integrated.

I remember when I first started Rebirthing and I was determined to do it exactly right in order to get results. It happened, but I discovered that when I gave up my expectations to get results, it happened even better. This taught me that there are no set rules to this process. As we began to work with the first four components, I further discovered that there was no need to apply them perfectly, or even try, to get wonderful results. Michael, my own teacher taught me something I have never forgotten:-

EXPECTATION LEADS TO EFFORT,
EFFORT LEADS TO STRUGGLE, AND
STRUGGLE LEADS TO PAIN!

Integration is always perfect and is much easier than suppression, the same as it is easier to 'succeed' at life than it is to 'fail', whatever those words mean. It is very hard work for the system to keep something suppressed, although we are not always aware of this strain on the body and mind along with the drain of energy from us. So if the circumstances for integration are roughly set up, then integration will happen.

The first four components are presented only as effective steps to how integration can best be achieved. But reality does not always go along with how things 'should be', even if they are proven. Occasionally integration will happen when we are controlling our breath, when we have lost our awareness, while finding an experience unpleasant, and possibly even when our muscles are tensed. Rebirthing is one of the safest and simplest techniques we can ever do, and because we don't have to do it right to make it work, it is safe to experiment. For example, if our Rebirther instructs us to breathe fast and shallow, but our intuition tells us to breathe slow and full, then do it that way. Since we are in a state of perfection before, during and after doing anything, how could we possibly do Rebirthing wrong? So relax into the process and it does not matter what happens during Rebirthing, because whatever happens is the right happening.

CHAPTER 7

THE REBIRTHING CYCLE

The technique of REBIRTHING can be described as a cycle.

1. CONSCIOUS CONNECTED BREATHING — which activates the suppressed energy.
2. FOCUSING AWARENESS — observing the energy in the greatest possible detail. Totally filling one's consciousness with it.
3. BLISS-CONSCIOUSNESS — totally accepting and loving every aspect of the experience.
4. TOTAL RELAXATION and surrender to the energy.
5. WHATEVER HAPPENS IS THE RIGHT HAPPENING.

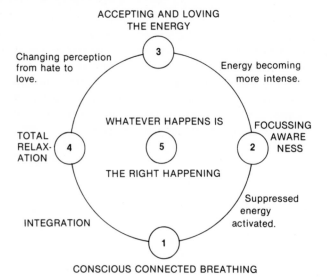

The diagram explains the typical REBIRTHING cycle. Each component, although described separately throughout this book, is part of the one over-all process.

When a Rebirthee masters the technique, the whole process (the five components) happen almost simultaneously. For example, after breathing for a time, and material begins to be activated, the Rebirthee focuses his awareness; affirms his love for the energy and enjoys it; and completely surrenders to it, almost all at the same time. Often the energy integrates very quickly at a subtle level, and a new cycle can begin. Mostly however, an experienced Rebirthee will often find that his REBIRTHING cycle will not resemble the diagram very much because all the components merge into the one process and another person observing will notice very little happening.

WHAT THE REBIRTHING PROCESS IS LIKE FOR BEGINNERS

The experience of rebirthing is unique for every person and for this reason, we can't really say how each session will go. No two sessions are ever the same because once a suppression has been integrated, it is gone forever. Thus, each new pattern of energy that surfaces can feel different. Some people will experience the process more intensely than others. Some will experience intense emotionality and sometimes the very emotion which accompanied the original act of suppression years before can be experienced. Some will experience early life memories which surrounded the act of suppressing.Most people will experience each of the above in varying degrees exclusive to themselves. Others may experience very little and think nothing much is happening at all. But whatever happens is the right happening and each person will work through exactly what is appropriate for them.

At the start the Rebirthee becomes aware of energy movements throughout the body. This may involve having memories, emotions, some tetany, and physical sensations like tingling or more intense feelings. These are signals that we are resisting our own healing which is perfectly normal, as we have probably been doing so all our lives. Just relax more. Most sessions end with you very relaxed and feeling just wonderful. As the suppressed energy is integrated, the Rebirthee begins to experience an inner peace, increased happiness, compassion and an expansion of awareness. This expansion of awareness, or consciousness, which many people report after the first few sessions, is quite different from the temporary acceleration of awareness which may come from the chemical stimulation of coffee or tea, or some more potent drug. Expansion of awareness is the result of clearing the physical, mental and emotional systems of suppressed energy enabling a person to maintain awareness more clearly and for more of the time.

During this time the Rebirthee is introduced to affirmations or possibly self observation techniques in order to extend the Rebirthing process to encompass all areas of their life.

As the process develops with later sessions, the more experienced Rebirthee will begin to operate more powerfully and at a more subtle level of consciousness. He or she will, in most cases, begin to feel their Inner Bliss as their system becomes clearer. The sessions will be even more pleasurable as confidence and experience in the process increases. During this time some Water Rebirthing Sessions could be a good idea, as well as some preparation for Self Rebirthing. Some Rebirthers run group Rebirthing Sessions, where several people are Rebirthing at the same time. These can be fun to attend and best attempted after completing at least ten Rebirthing sessions with the personal guidance of a qualified Rebirther.

HISTORY OF REBIRTHING

Rebirthing was developed in the early seventies by Leonard Orr in the United States. He first developed it as a hot water technique, which simulated the experience of being in the womb. It soon became clear that the water for the first few sessions activated so much material that it tended to overwhelm most people. So he devised the dry Rebirth. He discovered that it was the breathing and relaxing in the presence of a Rebirther that was crucial and not the water, as was thought originally. So, for a number of years, Rebirthing was taught

My personal introduction into Rebirthing, the training emphasis was focused mainly on the breath, with encouragement to dramatise feelings and give full expression to them.

Alot of Integration and healing took place, but with the discovery of the other four components, Rebirthing became more gentle, enjoyable and even more effective. People felt safer with a more gentle approach and therefore relaxed more into it, achieving Integration sooner.

It is not suggested here that Rebirthing is the only way to a grand and glorious future. We are suspicious of people who claim to have the only way. Nor does it interfere in any way with the benefits gained from any therapeutic, religious, or self development experiences practiced elsewhere. In fact, Rebirthing enhances these experiences.

The essence of improvement is change, but Rebirthing is about development. The difference is that improvement suggests to make better where development means to expand what already is there. How can we improve upon perfection; only that perfection needs developing in as much as it needs to be brought to the surface of the person's life for its expression. True Rebirthing is not in the self-improvement business, but rather is all about self-development. If any change is needed, it is for changes in attitudes and rebirthing makes such changes easier.

SOME ADDITIONAL POINTS A NEW REBIRTHEE SHOULD KNOW:

1. A REBIRTHER is someone who has worked out a large proportion of their earlier life traumas and is specifically trained in the technique.
2. A REBIRTHEE is someone who is willing to integrate their suppressions, and clear their systems.
3. THE REBIRTHEE takes full responsibility of his or her own Rebirthing process and for consequences of anything that happens during or after.
4. With this understanding, the REBIRTHER will assist and guide the REBIRTHEE through the process in any way they both feel appropriate.
5. So far Rebirthing has worked on everyone that has tried it. It is natural, safe and easy.
6. It is necessary to have a REBIRTHER to gain maximum benefit from the technique.

This last point is very important. The process works best when folk are assisted through with an experienced REBIRTHER.

I have written this, not as a training manual, but as an introduction to Rebirthing. No one can learn Rebirthing from a book. It can only be learnt with an experienced REBIRTHER. This will however, prepare anyone for their Rebirthing process.

CHAPTER 8

FOCUSING AWARENESS

The heart of total awareness is being conscious of the *present moment*. The ever present moment is a subject of such vital importance in the deliverance from pain and suffering, yet it is overlooked by so many scholars, philosophers, psychologists, religious folk, and those involved in healing. The principle of the eternal *present moment* is so vast that we will not do it justice here.

Basically, the aim is to bring our consciousness into the *present moment* and thus be aware of everything in the here and now to the greatest possible extent. It is expanding awareness to embrace all thoughts, all feelings and all sensations, as well as being aware of our external world, all at the same time. At first glance this may appear impossible for most of us. Few of us are able to make such a jump in consciousness to achieve such a feat of perfect integration. The main reason we can't is because of the numerous blocks and suppressions in the system, as well as a lack of development of 'Inner Essence'.

The 'Inner Essence' is the crystallization of the Truth within us, and its growth is inhibited while the system is clogged up.

It is impossible to suppress anything, to suffer anxiety, inadequacy, fear, jealously, anger, guilt, worry, rejection and even physical pain, while living one hundred percent in the *present moment*. We can feel any emotion or sensation including physical pain, but we do not suffer from them in that perfect time OF NOW.

All negative thoughts and feelings, which are created while living outside the the Present Moment, are caused by a condition of the mind called the 'ego'. The ego is something we have created out of fear and is the cause of all suffering. The ego is all that is false within us and is linked to either the past or the future.

Unhappiness simply cannot be experienced whilst being in the *now*. If you doubt it, then consider this; the next time you feel unhappy, look closely and you will see how it is connected to either something that has already happened in the past, or something you think will happen in the future. And if you are unhappy with a present condition or situation, again it is because you are comparing it with a more pleasant past memory, or a hopeful expectation of the future. The most enormous loss of happiness is a comparison with the past or expectation and fear of the future.

This is more easily proved through practise than by theory. By concentrating totally upon what is happening in the present moment, we will make a wonderful discovery. We will see that the ego does not even exist. The ego is only a collection of feelings, ideas, and thought patterns which lose their hold over us when we begin to enter the present moment. By concentrating completely upon a negative feeling, the ego is revealed by the light of Reality and the feeling begins to dissolve because it's support system of 'lies' (the ego) begins to disappear. Don't take my word for this: try it for yourself.

By concentrating solely upon the *now*, we are able to Integrate our past, and future, along with the ego and it's regrets, comparisons and pride of yesterday, and it's expectations, fears, and anxieties for tomorrow.

The ego is a prisoner of time, but as we come into the 'present moment' we are released from our attachments and anxieties, freed from our past and our future and liberated from our ego. The present moment is perfect freedom from our 'conditioned' ego.

The present moment is the only reality that exists. Yesterday does not exist except in our memory. Even one minute ago is gone forever. Five minutes from now does not exist except in our imagination.

Our perception of reality is blurred most of the time. If we are thinking negatively, or off daydreaming, or worrying and being fearful about future events, or resenting and regretting things that happened in the past, we are missing the most important moment in our entire life — 'THE PRESENT MOMENT'.

If we are not enjoying our present moment flow of consciousness, it is because of our emotional programming of demands, attachments and models of how life should treat us based on a dead past; or our desires and expectations based on an imagined future. They keep us from being here now, thus we experience the conditioned programming in our head instead of enjoying the now.

Our level of awareness is kept very limited and unfulfilled if we are controlled by 'pasting and futuring'. We become very much dominated by uncontrollable emotions which insist on pleasures of the past being re-enacted in the now; or by situations that support our expectations of how things should be. These ideas are only put to the test when things go wrong in our lives.

I remember one night early in 1983, I set off to an important meeting, and a mile from home my car got a puncture along a very dark and deserted country lane. I had stopped on a hill and in my hurry I'd forgotten to put the hand-brake on or leave the car in gear. I jumped out and quickly began changing the tyre in the dark without a torch. With the jack half-way up, the car began rolling down the hill. It didn't roll very far, but enough to wreck my jack which was a wind-up type. I picked up the twisted and now useless jack and for the first time in my life I really became aware of what was happening inside me. Firstly, my old conditioning came up accompanied with a rage that made me want to throw the jack clean through the windscreen. My conditioning and rage demanded someone or something be blamed. I mentally ran a check list at which to direct my anger: I first blamed the car, then the repair garage who had last serviced the car, then the dealer who had 'ripped me off' for selling me the car eighteen months earlier. Having exhausted this line, I became angry at the expected costs involved in repairing it, furious at the inconvenience of the car 'breaking down', also preventing me from attending my meeting and being stranded. I then realised that I had a choice of either going off the deep end and exploding all my frustrations to the surrounding trees, and achieving nothing except high blood-pressure or, alternatively accepting the situation as it was with humour and love. I chose to accept and love what was happening to me, and I changed my entire life in that instant. It was like a major revelation for me. 'I can choose to feel any way I like'. I'd heard this theory before, but it meant little to me until then, when I experienced it. I gently placed the jack next to the car and skipped home like a five year old singing along with beautiful happy, loving feelings.

I missed my meeting, but I gained a growth experience and a lesson so valuable that has helped me ever since. 'THE LESSON OF CHOICE'. To either hate a situation, to disown it, ignore it and suppress it, OR to love it, to accept and own it.

I could only have discovered this by centering myself in that present moment which freed me from a conditioned past. By tuning into the here and now I discovered that I can, always had, and always will, have enough to enjoy every moment in my life. Those times when I'm not in a state of bliss are because I have chosen to allow my programmed conditioning of the past or expectations of an imagined future to dominate my consciousness in the here and now. By being in the present moment we are able to accept what was once the unacceptable and keep our calm, our humour, and we use the experience to grow. The here and now is the gateway to Bliss-consciousness and cannot be realised until we are centered in the present moment.

When we are not in the present moment we are not connected with Reality (Truth). When we are not truthful to the present moment we begin to experience negative feelings which is the ego's resistance against Truth. The present moment connects with every area of our lives. Thousands of bed-ridden patients could heal themselves by understanding this secret. Psychosomatic illness of every kind starts from the pressure of trying to live in a different time span to that of the here and now.

A good affirmation to use:

'I have everything I need to enjoy my being here.'

It is easy to find fears we can mentally enlarge upon to support our conditioned structure of expectations and demands; alternatively, we can consciously choose to enjoy everything in our here and now. We always have enough to be truly happy if we are enjoying what we do have and are not worrying about what we don't have.

Unfortunately, the residue of our past, the things we made wrong because of our conditioning, colours our present moment and prevents us from living it. So we are not in touch with reality which is ecstasy. We know we are in touch with reality to the extent that we experience unconditional happiness in any given moment.

The present moment is perfect freedom from all that binds — all conditioning, all suppressions, all fixed ideas, all things that are not in harmony with perfect bliss.

People who brand these ideas that are being expressed here as idealistic with no relevance to the 'harsh real' world out there, are people who justify living the way they do. The thought of change is just too difficult to make. It is far easier to remain in that old familiar pattern of life, even though it is filled with tension and anxiety with patches of pleasure. Thirty or forty years of conditioning seems just too much to give up for some folk. Yet it is the only path to Eternal Ecstasy.

So, Rebirthing can be described as a technique which helps us break through the husk of old conditioning and suppressed patterns of energy, releasing us from the slavery of our past. This raises us up to a higher level of consciousness we call 'Bliss Consciousness', and where we experience ecstasy all the time.

Total awareness as it applies to Rebirthing, is focusing on sensations, and feelings, that come to our attention in the body. The patterns of energy we become aware of during Rebirthing are mostly physical sensations like tingling in the toes, fingers or face, to more intense energy patterns appearing anywhere. In fact they can be any physical sensation we have ever experienced, as well as any thought, emotion, memory, or whatever. When suppressed material becomes activated, we can sometimes experience the thoughts and especially the emotions we felt when we first suppressed that particular experience. However, we may not always experience such thoughts and emotions if we integrate the material at a subtle level.

During the course of Rebirthing sessions, the patterns of energy change. Suppressed material is like a husk surrounding our true self, and is in layers, one on top of each other like layers of an onion. When a layer integrates, the pattern of energy we felt has either disappeared or ceased to be important. As each layer integrates, it usually activates the next layer beneath it. As each layer is different, each Rebirthing session and experience within a session can be different. So we should never compare one session with another because in doing so, we begin to have expectations of how the next session should be. It doesn't work that way. Whatever happens or appears not to be happening is exactly the right happening for that time. As we become more experienced at Rebirthing, less and less appears to be happening. This is because we are operating at a finer level and therefore integrating suppressions at a more subtle level. It also means that we are clearing the system faster, more efficiently and of more material.

Sometimes, our awareness can be attracted to one, two and even three things which are coming up separately almost at the same time. This can happen when different parts of the one pattern of energy get activated separately. For example, if we are integrating a suppressed experience of having had a motor accident when we were young, first might come fear, then pain, and then anger. Then, in an integrative memory, it may all come at the same time. We should focus on the energy which is the strongest at such times, whether it be the physical pain or the emotion.

It sometimes happens that we suddenly become aware of things happening ouside, next door, or in the next room which seem to distract us. Our awareness can be drawn to these distractions because we are unconsciously avoiding an energy pattern beginning to be activated. Sometimes these energy patterns can be triggered off by the distraction and often we feel annoyed by them. At other times the distraction can come as an itch or a desire to move and fidget. Again, it is likely to be a pattern of energy coming up and we should focus on what is happening in the body and experience it in detail. Sounds of the local environment can help some folk to activate material, so it is better to be aware of external things rather than try to block them out.

It is helpful to remain aware of the whole physical body during the session. Of course, we will become more aware of certain things more than others, but whatever comes into our experience is exactly what we should focus on and experience totally at that moment.

LOSING AWARENESS

Losing awareness means anything that makes us unaware of the energy patterns in the body. Going to sleep is the most common example. Although it is important to completely relax in order to integrate material, it is also important to focus awareness onto the activated material so as to speed up, and integrate all of it.

SLEEP

Many people do experience going to sleep at some stage during a Rebirthing session. This often happens just after integrating something and the beautiful, relaxed feeling that accompanies integration once the load of carrying suppressions and stresses for so long has been lifted, makes a person 'drift-off' into a little sleep.

Some people who live frantic and stressful lives find that because deep relaxation is so foreign to them, the body grabs at the chance to relax and they go to sleep. Such people are often refreshed by a short nap and then the session can resume.

However, most people go to sleep during a Rebirthing session in order to avoid what the breathing is bringing up. It is an avoidance technique that the ego uses as a ploy. Integration is all about lessening the ego which is nothing more than a form of conditioning. As Rebirthing is all about removing conditioning, the ego becomes very tricky and mostly operates from the subconscious so we can not always take charge and prevent ourselves from going to sleep. That is why we need a Rebirther to help us through this small hindrance until we have mastered the process ourselves.

To overcome sleepiness we do Full and Fast Connected Breathing which brings us back to the body. Sitting up or kneeling on hands and knees, also helps to overcome sleepiness.

Losing awareness in Rebirthing can take other forms which are sometimes used to avoid what the breathing is activating. This avoidance behaviour is often subconscious and can include wanting to constantly talk to the Rebirther, wanting to act out the emotions that come up instead of relaxing into them, drifting off into thoughts and fantasies, suspending the breath, and for those who tend to be intellectual most of the time, a chronic lack of contact with physical sensations and emotional feelings.

COMMUNICATING DURING REBIRTHING

It is often necessary for the Rebirther and Rebirthee to communicate during a session. It is also a good idea for you as a Rebirthee to briefly express and verbalise what you are feeling physically and emotionally, but not all the time. This will help you to more readily focus in on the pattern of energy. It is also good to ask for things you feel you need which corresponds with where you are at, at any time during your Rebirthing. For instance, a blanket placed over you while curled up in the foetal position when integrating fear; a substitute teddy bear to cuddle up to; for your Rebirther to rub your back, stroke your hair, or hug you and so on. It's your Rebirthing session, so don't be afraid to ask for anything you feel will help the process.

Yet sometimes we may be more interested in talking than Rebirthing This avoidance technique can be conscious or even unconscious, and our Rebirther may gently remind us to breathe rather than talk.

ACTING OUT EMOTIONS

Although acting out a feeling does not cause integration, it can help us to focus in on the energy that is coming up. If we want to cry, go ahead and cry. If we want to curl up into a ball, then do so. These and other things we may want to do are perfectly correct during a session, so long as we are not doing them to avoid and distract us away from an energy pattern that we are choosing to feel uncomfortable about. Until we master the Bliss Principle, which is simply choosing to enjoy every experience that comes along, there can sometimes be a tendency to avoid or resist the energy pattern by acting out an emotion that is accompanying it. If we become aware that we are doing this, just remember that it is possible to enjoy anything, and then relax completely into the feelings and sensations and continue to breathe. Remember, expressing an emotion does not necessarily lead to integration.

DRIFTING OFF INTO THOUGHTS AND FANTASIES

Sometimes when we have just integrated something and we are feeling very good and relaxed, it is very easy to drift off onto a train of thoughts and fantasies. This happens a lot with people who like to analyse thoughts and situations, and for those who like to daydream. This may be very pleasurable to do and okay for a little while, but it costs us in lost awareness. If we have a brilliant idea that comes to us in the middle of a session, give the mind this instruction:
'Ten minutes after this Rebirthing session is over I will clearly remember this idea'.
Then begin to breathe fast and full.

SUSPENDING THE BREATH

This is when a person suddenly stops breathing during Rebirthing and appears to go unconscious. In fact, they are in a very deep state of consciousness, some people call a 'transcendental' state, or 'objective consciousness'. It can be best described as transcending, or going beyond the thoughts, the emotions, beyond sensations in the body. There is nothing dangerous or bad about experiencing this, in fact it is highly pleasurable and very beneficial. The suspended breath is in fact not a method to avoid anything the breathing is bringing up, but another form of integrating material at a very subtle level.

It happens when a person has reached a very deep state of relaxation after having performed connected breathing deeply for quite a while. The blood is rich in oxygen, the system has probably just been cleared of some suppressed energy, and suddenly, the whole system goes into a state of almost suspended animation. The mind, the emotions and the body virtually close down except for a very faint heart beat. This is regarded by many as the ultimate state of relaxation. Some people have been known to remain in this state for up to five minutes, and they do not respond even to loud noises or being shaken. There is no danger that the person will not come out of this highly delightful state because the body's own survival mechanism automatically starts the system working again when it's ready.

Some rebirthees do not remember experiencing the suspended breath, while others report early childhood memories, and others seem to have certain psychic experiences. Some remember all of it and others remember nothing. Most however, report a profound feeling of safety, complete relaxation and sheer ecstasy afterwards, while during the suspended breath period, they have no recollection at all.

Not everyone experiences suspending the breath, particularly those who try to experience it, for it happens unexpectedly when all conditions of the system are just right for it. Those who never experience it still get as much benefit from Rebirthing as those who do experience it. It is simply an added bonus for those who do.

The experience of the suspended breath can be best described like this. We know that we have had it, but we don't know we are having it. We are not asleep, nor having thoughts, feelings or sensations, as we have gone beyond all experiences to briefly touch our Inner Self.

LACK OF CONTACT WITH PHYSICAL AND EMOTIONAL FEELINGS

Intellectual people tend to lack physical sensations and emotional feelings, because their centre of gravity is in their head. They still feel things on these levels, but their awareness is not as acute in the body or their emotions as say an emotional person or a busy active person, whose centre of gravity lies in different areas.

Then there are people who are so suppressive that they don't feel anything irrespective of being emotional or physical.

Intellectuals and suppressive folk have the most to gain from Rebirthing. Because Rebirthing requires that most of the activated energy be made aware of through feeling, these people can often be the most challenging to Rebirth.

If you ask them how they feel, or what they are feeling, they will answer in terms of the kind of thoughts they are having, yet they will call them feelings. Most other people will be able to answer in terms of a certain kind of feeling or sensation in some part of their body.

It is possible for all of us to always feel something physically, and it is necessary in Rebirthing to do so. All the time there is something happening in the body, the moving of energy from one part to another, the heart-beat, the flow of blood around the body and so on. We don't have to wait for the breathing to activate something during a session to focus our awareness or be totally aware (the second component). So when we *think* there is nothing happening during our Rebirthing session, we have lost our self-awareness and are deluding ourselves, because there is *always* something happening. In training ourselves to be self-aware we are more able to focus in on activated material while it is still subtle, thus integrate it early and make the whole experience highly pleasurable. Although ignoring a pattern of energy until it gets very intense is still effective, it takes some of the pleasure out of the experience.

That which is most familiar to us is often the most difficult to become aware of. Our stress, for instance, is something we have lived with for so long that we simply don't feel it. We don't notice it because we have suppressed it, withdrawn our awareness away from it. Often, our most deeply held and most important patterns of suppressed material are the most difficult to get in touch with, for the same reason that we are often unaware of our breathing during the day. We all breathe continuously without giving any thought to breathing. We simply do it without being aware of it, until we go under water for instance, or do breathing as a growth technique, like Rebirthing.

In Leonard Orr and Sondra Ray's book, "Rebirthing in the New Age", they write:

"Memory blocks caused by past traumatic experiences are a common subject of psychology. The theory is that painful experiences are blocked from the memory because the person does not want to remember the pain. Our theory is that remembering the experience releases the pain and frees the mind and body; and that the release is not painful, but sometimes intensely pleasurable. The fear of painful memories holds the pain in the mind or body to be experienced as pain or tension. To free your memory you have to get rid of the concept that remembering painful incidents makes the pain worse; and you have to get into the idea that the release is worth the time — and wonderful.

Rebirthing is focused on releasing rather than re-experiencing the trauma. Most people, when taking out their household garbage, don't find it necessary to examine each individual can, bottle, wrapper and box before discarding it. However, it is a curious phenomemon that those same people, before letting go of any 'psychological garbage' will find it necessary to meticulously pick through, sift, taste, touch, smell, analyse, classify, examine, and understand each item in order to make sure they don't throw out anything valuable. Using this analogy, we say that if psychoanalysis and psychotherapy are like diligently picking through your psychological garbage in an attempt to understand it, then Rebirthing (in most cases) is like carrying out your garbage in one fell swoop. In the beginning some people find this very disconcerting, because the Rebirthing process releases negative mental mass so quickly you don't have time to think about or understand it. After the Rebirth, however, most people are so high and feel so good that they could not care less about 'understanding' it.''.

This sums up our concept of total awareness. We need only be aware of the present moment experience. Whatever our Rebirthing is bringing up, be totally aware of it and this speeds up integration. Whatever our life situations are presenting us with, be totally aware of it and this will develop our acceptance and compassion.

CHAPTER 9

BLISS CONSCIOUSNESS

The idea of Bliss Consciousness is the main philosophy behind Rebirthing. In fact, it is the philosophy behind all the great teachings except that it seems to have been lost somehow, or has been reduced to a superficial mythical concept of punishment or reward like Heaven or Hell, Karma or such like.

These concepts of cause and effect are very real but are limited to the mind in this plane of existence. Higher levels of consciousness known as 'Self Realisation' goes beyond these self-limiting levels of consciousness to transcend the very fountainhead of thought and understanding and to arrive at Truth itself.

Bliss Consciousness refers to a state of consciousness quite beyond the ordinary state of awareness most of us experience every day. The concept of Bliss Consciousness is presented as a belief system until we actually experience It, then It becomes reality: this belief system is that *we are in a state of perfect bliss whether we are consciously aware of it or not.* This is the Truth within each of us. That spark of Divinity which unites all humankind. When this Truth comes into the conscious level of mind, we experience Bliss Consciousness at that level. Until then, this state remains at the subconscious level, waiting for us to integrate it into our surface consciousness, by clearing the falseness from our lives. Falseness is not real. It is an illusion. Only Truth is reality and when we are in touch with Truth we experience Bliss.

When we are untruthful to the present moment by not being here now, we separate ourselves from Truth and suffer the loss of bliss on the conscious level by making it subconscious. It is a form of lying to ourselves. We are denying the Truth that is before us in the Now situation by dwelling in either the past or the future. A situation is made wrong by withdrawing awareness away from Truth, which is a lie (an untruth). When awareness is withdrawn from something we ignore it, and ignorance is what is left. Ignorance is the cause of all suffering.

Instinctively, however, we know that Bliss Consciousness exists, or we would not be continually searching for It and happiness in our lives. In an attempt to find our original nature, which is Ecstasy, we seek out pleasure outside ourselves. Yet we are only temporarily satisfied because all things are constantly changing. Only Truth is constant.

Finding truth is the art of discovering the very fountainhead of all Ecstasy which is within our being and not in exterior attractions. Pleasure coming from exterior things is conditional. All bliss coming from within is unconditional and therefore is constantly present, whether we consciously experience it or not, while the joy which comes from outside us does so only in appearance and not in reality. No amount of wealth, power, sex, drugs, fine food, and so on contain happiness in themselves, but only serve to draw out a minute portion of that Infinite Bliss latent within each of us. This is proved by the fact that what pleases one person, does not necessarily do so for someone else. One person may find temporary satisfaction in sex and power, but may be indifferent to food and drugs; another person may find that getting approval is all important. Yet another will find pleasure in money, material possessions and so on. If true happiness lay inherent in all these things instead of within each person, then there would be no difference in the taste of the passing pleasures, but complete uniformity instead.

Bliss is the underlying state, constantly present, whereas the experience of happiness is an impression gained by the mind when our thought processes make contact with some pleasant memory or object. For example, we see a flower or an object of beauty — the contact of the sight with the object produces an impression on the mind as a feeling of happiness. But this happiness is conditional because it is based on emotional demands and expectations. Take away the object of beauty and the happiness may also disappear.

The experience of Bliss is there regardless of whatever the thought processes make contact with. Bliss is not dependent on a continuous supply of 'groovy' sensations, or sights of beauty to induce happiness. It is always there regardless.

Most of us do not experience this. Why? It is because of the state of our mind. It is all clogged up with suppressions and tensions. Until we have cleared the system, our experience of happiness is probably by way of feelings of emotions, physical sensations, or intellectual amusements. At our level, the degree of happiness produced by an impression which goes into the mind depends upon the purity of the mind; while a purer mind, that is a mind that is uncluttered with stress etc., enjoys more out of the experience of the same object.

For example, when the senses come in contact with an object, they produce an impression of the object in the mind, and the creation of the impression, while producing the sensation of experience, simultaneously produces feelings and emotions of happiness or unhappiness. In other words, the more blocks we have within us, the more dreary our world appears. The clearer our system is, the more beautiful our world is.

As we clear the system, our consciousness expands, and the capacity of experiencing and understanding things on a deeper level happens naturally. With growth, the ability of experiencing greater happiness and understanding increase simultaneously. For example, we see a flower and we feel happy. But the happiness we feel is on the basis of our capacity for happiness. As our consciousness expands, our capacity for happiness increases. With this increased capacity we see the same flower and therefore we enjoy it more.

The capacity to enjoy every experience is the secret to the Bliss Principle. But by separating ourselves from the Truth by insisting that an experience is unpleasant, we limit our capacity for happiness by losing some of our awareness. We have chosen to make an experience wrong by closing off the awareness with an untruth that something is unpleasant. Nothing in the universe is wrong or unpleasant. It is all perfect Ecstasy. But if we insist that something is unpleasant, then we set up a value system of good and bad, right and wrong, pleasure and suffering, conscious and subconscious. This belief in duality is the cause of suffering, because it is based on ignorance.

Many people have trouble on first coming in contact with the Bliss Principle, and I must admit, so did I. For instance, people ask how can you bliss-out on seeing crime, rape, violence and war? How can there be balance in the world without evil and only good? For example, there is a widespread belief that it is the two equal opposing forces of good and evil, positive and negative, yin and yang and so on, that hold the universe in balance, and without one or the other the universe would dissolve. This may be true.

However, when our vision is focused upon the lower levels of consciousness and our attachment is confined to the earthly field of existence, we remain bound within those limitations.

We need to raise our sights to higher fields of existence. For example, imagine a pendulum swinging from left to right and the right represents good, while the left represents evil. If we focus on the right and love only the good while hating and denying the evil, we are dividing the manifested creation into a duality experience. But by expanding our consciousness to embrace the high point — the pivot on which the pendulum swings — we will find perfect stillness, balance and harmony. This is the destiny of all humankind — to find that inner peace, love and perfection. That apex of life which is the divinity in all of us. That higher self that is perfect and joyful, whether we are aware of it or not.

The reason we have crime, rape, violence and war is due to hatred and greed. One man sees another man or nation which has more than he has and so he feels jealous. Jealousy turns to hatred and so he takes up a gun to destory that which he hates. The Catholics and Protestants in Northern Ireland see the other side with hatred, something that must be eliminated, and so with hate in their hearts they try to destroy each other. This is the same wherever men divide themselves from each other with hate.

Hatred and jealousy basically stem from fear and fear is the result of suppression. When we have suppressed energy, we become conditioned by an ego which feels separate from other people. This separation is the only evil that exists and the word 'evil' is just the same word as 'Live' except that it is spelt backwards.

As Mahatma Gandhi once said, "The only devils that exist are those that run around in the hearts of men".

Once I had an acquaintance I'll call Peter, who was a very dedicated Christian, except that his personal doctrine seemed to be a doctrine of non-acceptance rather than the one of love that Jesus taught. He seemed to be obsessed with the idea of 'the work of the devil'. Crime, war, disasters, famine, etc., were all the works of Satan. He often warned me that I should 'beware' because of my 'new age' thinking, as the Prince of Darkness would possess me. Yet I observed Peter and found that he was very intolerant of people's weaknesses and continually asserted that unless you repented and admitted you were a 'sinner', you would be damned in the eternal fires of Hell forever. Peter's intolerance of 'weaker' persons, which seemed to include almost everyone except himself, eventually caused him to despise most people. He even began to take on the physical characteristics of that which he hated the most — the devil. It seemed that he was manifesting what was mostly on his mind. I last heard that Peter was undergoing psychiatric treatment. Incidentally, I have found the same fanaticism in many other religions and some political philosophies. This intolerance might have something to do with why many different groups are killing each other in different parts of the world.

Jesus, along with Buddha, Krishna, Mohammed and all the great teachers, taught Oneness and Love, and that ignorance created a false self which was referred to as evil or the devil. It seems that many devotees and followers of these teachers have perverted the teaching by giving false power to ignorance by creating a devil as a real and separate entity.

Of course, belief in a separate entity, which we can call evil and blame all our misfortunes on, suits our ego very well. It enables us to avoid any responsibility for our lives. Belief in this non-existent falseness or ego which manifests itself as certain thoughts and feelings is what makes us think we are separate from truth, and therefore helps us make things wrong by living in duality.

In the Bhagavad Gita, Chapter 7:27, it is written, "O, brave Arjuna! Man lives in a fairy world, deceived by the glamour of opposite sensations, infatuated by desire and aversion."

By living a life of opposites, we crave for happiness, but by believing in unhappiness, we experience it. By living a life of opposites we crave pleasure, but by believing in suffering, we experience it. This applies to any belief in anything false. Through ignorance, by living a life of opposites, we swing from likes and dislikes, attractions and repulsions, attachments and aversions, peace and anxiety, love and hate, Heaven and Hell, past and future, which in their turn keep up a whole series of delusion-ignorance-egoity of action and reaction.

All is perfect Bliss, whether we are consciously aware of it or not. But, because of our unawareness, we separate ourselves from the truth and live in a duality experience.

The amount of suffering in our lives depends on how much falseness or lying we are living by. We are creatures of habit and through conditioning in our upbringing, influences, etc. and self-feeding lies, we condition ourselves into a belief that we need things outside ourselves. Yet, in needing objects outside ourselves, we create an experience which is always accompanied with a belief that things can also hurt us. If we need things outside ourselves to give us happiness, the law is that we also create an unhappiness. This again is only an illusion of perception. We are so separated from truth which supplies our every need and shows us how complete we are in ourselves, that we become addicted to outside attractions. If these outside addictions and programmed conditionings are denied us, we suffer their loss until they are replaced or we are temporarily satisfied with another addiction. So an addiction is something we condition ourselves into believing we need, which in all cases is simply not true.

Humankind needs air, food, water, warmth and shelter to survive. We need truth, love, peace, laughter and knowledge to grow, which are all contained within us, and other people may be needed to open the inner doorway to find these treasures of self-realisation. All else are wants which are good to experience, but often become a hindrance to a person's growth if he is trapped by being addicted to any of them.

The Buddha spoke of desire as the cause of all suffering. At our level he was referring to being addicted to anything outside ourselves. There is nothing wrong in wanting things, but if we suffer anxiety and stress when our wants are denied us, then we have an addiction, which is illusory.

Suffering itself is not illusory; for anxiety, loneliness, rejection, anger, fear and so on are real emotions and experiences. But their causes are illusory. If we suffer from fear of losing someone or something, that is illusion caused by not seeing the sufficiency of our own true nature.

We have all experienced fear which turned out to be unfounded. For instance, many of us have probably walked down a dark street at night and suddenly thought we could see a figure of a person waiting to pounce on us. Feeling very frightened, but on approaching and realising the figure to be merely a dustbin or tree, causes the illusions of the would-be-attacker to vanish along with our fears.

The cause of suffering is illusory because suffering can be dissolved by seeing our addictions and realising that our subconscious mind, where all our programmed conditioning and addictions have their roots, controls our surface consciousness. I use the word 'control' because control suggests using energy to suppress and hold in check. The subconscious mind controls the conscious mind and therefore we are slaves to the subconscious.

The subconscious mind means under-conscious, something that is beneath and outside our normal area of awareness. We are aware of our conscious mind but not of our subconscious mind. This is because the very first time we suppressed something and withdrew our awareness away from a part of creation, we separated ourselves from Truth, and created subconsciousness. The subconscious mind did not exist until we created it by making something wrong. Everytime we withdraw awareness away from something and suppress it, we enlarge the subconscious mind further at the expense of our aware conscious mind. When we deny the truth by insisting that something is unpleasant and make it subconscious, we limit our consciousness and self-awareness further and further. This is the 'darkness' referred to in the New Testament. By withdrawing awareness from any experience we tell ourselves is bad, we shrink the conscious mind into subconsciousness and darkness.

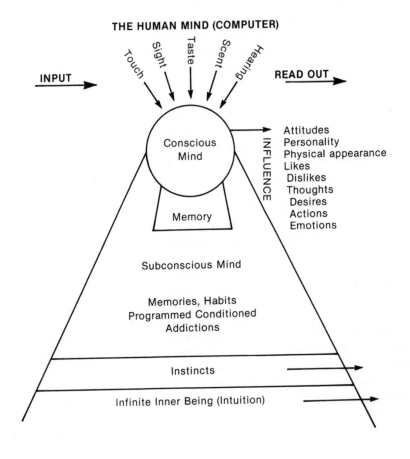

THE HUMAN MIND (COMPUTER)

SUBCONSCIOUS

Many psychologists, and inspirational writers refer to the subconscious as the seat of all inner power. In fact it is the seat of all our weaknesses. What they are really talking about is Infinite Intelligence beneath the subconscious. It is the subconscious which has covered over our inner strength, blocking its flow, making consciousness unconscious wherein ignorance prevails.

When we begin to centre ourselves through various techniques like Rebirthing, yoga, meditation and so on, our Essence, or Infinite Inner Being, begins to crystalise and express itself. As our Inner Being, which is the unconditional Bliss within, becomes more prominent, It begins to influence our outer being more and more.

The subconscious mind is symbolised in Christianity as 'original sin'. Adam is symbolic of the ego and the act of disobeying God is symbolic of denying the Truth and falling into ignorance/knowledge (conditioned beliefs). Way back at some stage, a spark of consciousness decided it wanted a part of creation all to itself without regard to any form of consciousness. So it separated itself from the One and became the Many. This act of greed created the first unconsciousness or subconsciousness, because awareness was withdrawn from Truth, and is symbolised by the casting out of Heaven of Satan and his angels.

Ignorance is a form of psychic sleep and everyone has a choice, to sleep or work on his or her Inner Self and eliminate the conditioned subconscious mind.

In 1978 I asked my teacher, Michael Freedman, the Senior Guardian of a Qabalistic Order, "what exactly is the subconscious mind?" Michael is a psychologist with Honours and a mystic with over 30 years experience in teaching meditation and consciousness expansion work. His answer baffled me for years when he said, "you figure it out. But I'll tell you this much. There is no beast as a subconscious mind as such. Only deeper consciousness." It took me five years to finally figure out that I had created my own subconscious by making something wrong by suppressing it and thus cutting off a slice of my consciousness, which became subconscious or unconscious. I only discovered this after fully realising that all my thoughts are creative. I create my world by my thoughts, which create my perception and how I perceive. Thus, if I perceive something and call it bad and ignore it, it becomes ignorance and subconscious. It remains in a subconscious condition which is held in a 'controlled' suppressed state until it is eventually integrated into consciousness through Rebirthing, meditation or some other centering or consciousness expansion work.

There is nothing bad, horrible, evil, wrong, or even unpleasant in the Universe. Everything is perfect. It is only our perception (ego) which sees things as bad, horrible, evil, wrong or unpleasant. Truth is perfect — and everything in existence comes from Truth and therefore must also be perfect. If it wasn't it would not have been created.

The only evil in the universe is negative thoughts, which make us perceive the Truth of existence as wrong. Yet, even negative thoughts are not wrong or evil in themselves, but simply act as a veil, preventing us from seeing Truth. Nothing can ever be wrong. This applies to every particle of matter, every thought, every bit of space and time. *This means that everybody is in the right place doing the right thing at the right time.* That is Truth.

When we make something wrong, we deny this truth and enslave ourselves. At this point, the act of actually suppressing some experience becomes subconscious, and so we have no recall or memory of how or why we did so. That is why when we integrate some suppressed material, we sometimes remember things way back in our early life. A part of the subconscious has become conscious again. Most of us have grown a subconscious so large, that we are unaware most of the time, lost in our thoughts and daydreams. By accepting and loving all that exists in our present moment, and taking full responsibility for everything in our experience being exactly the way it is, we are expanding our awareness, beginning to integrate the subconscious and aligning ourselves with Truth. We begin to know consciously that we are a part of the Creator of the Universe.

A good affirmation to use is:-
'' All experience is perfect joy.''
Fall asleep at night with this thought and let it be your first waking thought in the morning.

Another good affirmation is:-
"I love everything I experience in my here and now as part of my growth and pleasure."

As our consciousness expands, we begin to realise that we influence and help create the consciousness of everyone around us. That they play a reciprocal part in shaping the contents of our consciousness also. This feedback of awareness either enslaves us or frees us, depending on how self-aware we are. If we are free of blocks and addictions, we tend to help to free others of their blocks and addictions.

Since our consciousness creates our universe, by changing our point of view and our consciousness, we change our universe.

A loving person lives in a loving world because their gentle accepting awareness is mirrored by the same qualities in the people around them.

Similarly a hostile person lives in a hostile world. Everyone is regarded as a competitor, and under a thin layer of politeness a conditioned, simmering pot of anger, resentment, demands and expectations wait to boil over when things turn out differently from that which was expected. His actions provoke reactions from people around him and his world is angry.

The world is our mirror. The negativities we see in others are the very negativities we have in ourselves. Of course many people would deny this. Also the qualities we see in others are the qualities we also have, even though they may not be very developed.

The people I dislike the most are those that are so like me, with the same negative traits. I have learn't to overcome some of these negativities in myself by learning to love these people. They have been my best teachers because they were my mirror.

The study of the subconscious mind also highlights another important tendency in humans, and that is in the area of receiving communications. For example, if we have fixed ideas of how the world should be, that is, conditioned in certain thoughts and beliefs, then when someone talks to us about things that oppose our views, we totally screen out and reject what's coming in. We may be hearing the words, but our subconscious suppresses the information because they are threatening to our old structure of belief. A Self-Realised person feels no such threat, for having no subconscious, he or she is One with Truth and knows that Truth does not need defending, for it will stand on It's own.

Through our blindness of subconsciousness, we as humans, have separated ourselves into different religions, political beliefs, economic structures, philosophical approaches as well as from truth. We have not learnt that we are all one of the same in Essence. We have created a subconscious mind that not only separates us from Truth, but also from each other. There lies the answer to true and everlasting happiness, for it cannot exist in the darkness of separation and ignorance. It can only exist by integrating the subconscious mind into full and self-aware consciousness.

The object of Self-Realisation, Enlightenment, Salvation or whatever term we might like to use to find Eternal Bliss or God, is to first expand the conscious mind into the subconscious by the various

methods already talked about. This not only reveals all our programmed, conditioned addictions, which enables us to integrate them, but
also enables us to recall every memory in this life-time and possibly
beyond. The second step, once we have cleared the system of blocks
and suppressions, is to expand our consciousness to embrace the
Infinite Inner Being, and become One with the Absolute. This is
symbolised by the words in Isaiah 40:3, 'A voice cries: In this wilderness prepare ye the way of the Lord. Make straight in the desert a
highway for our God. Every valley shall be lifted up, and every
mountain and hill be made low; the crooked shall be made straight
and the rough places a plain. And the glory of the Lord shall be revealed, and all flesh shall see it together for the mouth of the Lord has
spoken.'

During the translation of this piece of esoteric scripture by theo-
logical scholars into Matthew 3:3 (which is supposed to be prophesy-
ing the coming of John the Baptist, the voice crying in the wilderness),
the scripture has become distorted, leaving an exoteric, surface understanding of what Isaiah was speaking of.

A voice cries (Infinite Inner Being); in this wilderness (subconscious); prepare ye the way of the Lord (expanding self-awareness); make straight in the desert (the mind); a highway for our God
(self-realisation).

Quite possibly Isaiah was foretelling the coming of John the Baptist. But compare the two writings translated in the same Bible by the
same scholars, (revised standard version).

Matthew 3:3 "The voice of one crying in the wilderness: prepare ye
the way of the Lord."

Isaiah 30:3 "A voice cries; In the wilderness prepare the way of the
Lord... For the mouth of the Lord has spoken."

The comparison shows that because of the break in the sentence
of Isaiah "A voice cries: In the wilderness, etc." and in Matthew,
"The voice of one crying in the wilderness, etc.", this slight change
in the sentence structure throws a complete and different meaning
between the two writings. More importantly, in Isaiah, Verse 5"...for
the mouth of the Lord has spoken" shows that the God within us is
speaking and not John the Baptist.

This is not a challenge to Matthew's reportings, because I am sure
his original text revealed the esoteric meanings as well as possibly

tying up the foretelling of John the Baptist in Isaiah. However a distinct loss of the deeper meaning through the numerous translations from Hebrew to Greek to Latin and eventually into English seems to have resulted.

Isaiah was speaking in a spiritual context of the wilderness of the mind, the desert within us and that we have created a subconscious mind; not about a landscape of a desert out in the wilderness. The original was the esoteric or hidden meaning of Isaiah, and the translation in Matthew's Gospel changed into exoteric surface understanding.

This diagram shows that as we expand our consciousness, we are automatically eliminating the subconscious. The subconscious is where all our conditioning lies and on integrating it all, our Path becomes straight toward reconnecting our surface consciousness with Infinite Inner being.

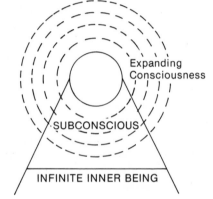

Wisdom is making the mind One with the unconditional bliss that lies within and which is the reality in contrast to the illusion of different minds.

The mind needs only to be cleansed and purified of all conditioning by simply accepting, enjoying and loving every aspect of it. Love purifies it all. Hate and fear are what created suppressions in the first place. The mind needs to be purified of conditioning in order to contain a perfect reflection of our Infinite Inner Being, in the same way that a dew drop must be free of dust in order to contain a perfect reflection of the sun. Our Infinite Inner Being is the Ecstasy centre and the purified mind simply reflects It like a mirror.

Stress and suppressions cause blocks in the mind's ability to reflect this Truth within us and should be integrated by loving it as the dust from a mirror is removed by the hand of the polisher. For specks of dust on the mirror of the mind are the suppressions and energy blocks which are created by the illusions of the mind in looking at life through the darkness of the subconscious. For what else is stress than the absence of relaxation, or unhappiness, than the absence of love and joy; as darkness is nothing but the absence of light. All unhappiness is nothing more than illusion we create in the mind, by believing such illusions exist as realities. When we close the blinds in a room, we shut out the sun and may believe that the sun no longer exists, even though in truth it continues to shine outside. We may believe in unhappiness and give a non-existing idea false power to dazzle us with illusory ideas. Yet we know that opening the blinds in our room to the light of the sun, removes all darkness, just as the person who opens the blinds of his or her mind to the Ecstasy of Infinite Inner Being removes all stresses and unhappiness.

No object outside ourselves contains happiness in itself, any more than any object or train of circumstances, whatever they may be, contains unhappiness in itself. To know this at a conscious level is one of the first and most valuable of all lessons in life, for it begins to clear a person of every illusion and suppression and eventually frees him. In deeper consciousness every one of us instinctively knows this anyway. We merely have to clear ourselves enough to begin to see it.

FEELINGS OF UNHAPPINESS ARE CAUSED BY COMPARING ONE EXPERIENCE WITH ANOTHER

We feel unhappy when we compare our present state with that of a past state, perhaps when we were younger or healthier, with another person, or had certain public honours, or reputation. When we live on the level of jealousy, we look out and see most other people as younger or better or richer or more attractive, which arouses our jealousy. Jealousy, like all other separating emotions, is another conditioned programmed addiction.

It is the same if we compare a small cottage to a large mansion. The cottage will seem small and inadequate. But if we compare the cottage only to itself, it will appear to be what it is, a warm, cosy shelter from the storm.

Similarly, in Rebirthing, if we experience an intense emotion or energy in some part of the body and compare it to what our feelings or body feels like usually, it will seem painful. If what is happening in our body is compared only to itself, we will see it as it really is, a perfectly enjoyable experience of the flow of energy in that part of the body. Intense pain in this context is just intense energy, and to regard it as unpleasant is to make it wrong. By surrendering to any experience that is happening in the physical body and comparing it only to itself is intense pleasure rather than intense pain.

Most of us associate going to the dentist with pain. We have probably always believed it to be unpleasant when we think of the drill or injection. But like all our addictions, it is a learned and conditioned reaction. By comparing it only to itself, we can choose to make it a pleasant and exciting experience. By associating the sensation of the drill boring into a tooth with being here now, in a state of perfect bliss and relaxing into it, we feel the energy as highly pleasurable.

When I first learned this idea, I had a chance to try it out with a trip to my dentist. I refused the injection for a filling that needed doing. I relaxed myself completely and kept telling myself that this drilling was highly pleasurable. Then he hit a nerve and my first reaction was "Oh, pain". I quickly centred myself, relaxed and kept affirming to myself that this really was pleasurable. And it worked. I actually began to enjoy it. Then he hit another nerve and I lost my self-awareness and my mind became flooded with negative thoughts. The intense energy became intense pain.

My next appointment two weeks later gave me the chance to try again. This time I held my self-awareness, my relaxation and the pleasure of it all for most of the session. I lost it near the end because my past programmed conditioning about dentists still needed clearing out, but I had made great progress. I have used this technique often since and it gets easier each time.

Most people on first hearing this idea are skeptical. They often say that they can think about pleasure all they want, but they still get unhappy when they feel pain. Or they may try it once and use their initial inability as the reason for giving up.

Think back to when we learned a new skill like driving a car or typing, or even Rebirthing. When did we believe that we could do it properly? A thought becomes a belief and then a reality when we have worked on it repeatedly, rather than simply trying a new idea once and then rejecting it because it did not work. Taking charge of our mental world requires determination to be happy in the here and now and to challenge and integrate each and every thought which tells us that feelings are bad or painful. All pain and all suffering is nothing more than intense energy warning us that something needs our attention. Pain in this context is just intense energy, and calling it pain means that we are making it wrong. By focusing our awareness on the intense energy, relaxing or surrendering completely to it, comparing it only with itself and breathing into it, we will experience intense pleasure instead of intense pain. This is the secret of overcoming pain, discomfort and every negative conditioned addiction we once labelled as bad or suffering.

Remember, pain or pleasure is only our interpretation. We need to change our state of consciousness to one in which we interpret every momentary experience as providing the most intense pleasure we have ever experienced. In this way, all experiences provide the ultimate joy and there is no comparison to give the illusion of greater or lesser pleasure or pain. When we develop beyond the duality of good and bad, pleasant and unpleasant, like and dislike, right and wrong, we will discover that fun and pain are all the same.

Every moment we live in the here and now is the most important moment in our entire life. If it wasn't, then we would be living the moment that was.

A good affirmation to use to bring us into the present moment to put us in touch with Truth is:

This is the most important moment in my entire life, so I am going to enjoy every aspect of it.

LOVE EVERY EXPERIENCE UNCONDITIONALLY

It's impossible to make something wrong when we love it unconditionally.

Animals are very receptive to human love and respond positively. There are numerous cases of wild animals appearing quite tame because some human had no fear and only love for animals.

Equally, animals pick up fear as strongly as love. Fear tells them that someone hates them and intends to harm them and so they attack simply out of self preservation.

Heather Barben, a dear friend of mine, was attacked by a rapist while she slept in her bed one night. There had been a number of reported rapes in the area over the preceding weeks. She suddenly woke up in the middle of the night with her attacker smothering her with his hand, preventing her from screaming and holding a knife to her throat. Coming out of a deep sleep and realising the crisis situation, she spontaneously prayed for the safety and protection not only of herself but also of her attacker. In spite of the situation she knew that he needed help as much as she did at that moment. She ceased struggling against him and they both began to calm down. Still sending loving protection for both of them, she became less afraid and his aggressiveness began to diminish as he felt less threatened and he even began to be more considerate towards her.

Heather later explained to me that as she gently talked to him, she felt only love and compassion for this terribly distressed and suffering human being, and wanted to nurture him as her fear and anger disappeared, and the whole situation began to defuse. After an hour of talking and showing him she neither feared nor hated him, he left without raping her or hurting her further. By overcoming her fear she saved herself and him through the power of love.

By loving every moment of our life no matter what, we become free of every block of suppressed energy inside us and tend to free others as well.

During a Rebirthing session, by loving every pattern of energy that is activated and which feels very intense, we extend our consciousness to the ecstasy of perfection.

The true meaning of life is found in the love and joy of celebrating every aspect of it. The concept that everything is perfect, that the universe is perfect and that we are perfect and in a state of total bliss, whether we are aware of it or not, may challenge many of the ideas we have been fed or superficially observed. But to think otherwise is to make a perfect situation 'wrong' and those feelings of depression, anxiety and pain are our resistance to truth and a message to correct our faulty thought patterns and conditionings.

GEMS ALONG THE WAY

- We are in a state of Bliss whether we are aware of it or not.
- Truth is being truthful to the present moment and living in the here and now.
- Bliss is found in truth and truth is within each of us.
- Ignorance is living a duality of suffering and joy, good and bad, likes and dislikes, love and hate, etc.
- No experience is bad or wrong. It is perfect joy unless we make it wrong by denying it.
- The subconscious mind did not exist until we created it by suppressing an experience.
- Everyone is in the right place doing the right thing at the right time.
- All experience is perfect joy.
- The world and everyone in it is our mirror.
- Feelings of unhappiness are created when we compare one experience with another.
- The true meaning of life is found in the love and joy of celebrating every aspect of it.

CHAPTER 10

DON QUIXOTE

The story of Don Quixote, as portrayed in a musical production of 'Man of La-Mancha' I once saw some years back, influenced me greatly when I was first putting my philosophy of life together.

'Man of La-Mancha' is a story about a supposedly deluded old man who believed that life should be lived not as it appears or is, but lived how it should be.

Living in seventeenth century Spain, the story goes that a man in prison waiting for trial on a heresy charge, decided to show his fellow prisoners that life is worth living, even while in a dungeon waiting to be tortured and possibly put to death by the Inquisition. This man put on a play by recruiting other prisoners in a portrayal of an inspiring, yet foolish appearing person called Don Quixote.

Don Quixote, after reading numerous books about knights and tales of chivalry, purchased himself an old rusted suit of armour, sword, lance and a boney old horse; recruited a friend called Sancho Panza who agreed to become his squire. So they sallied forth to banish the 'wicked' and fight for righteousness, glory, for God and country.

In the early part of his quest, Quixote was confronted with evil giants who suspiciously resembled windmills, but with courage and righteousness on his side he attacks but was unfortunately defeated suffering a broken sword, lance and a few bruises.

Never-the-less, he will one day return and defeat the tyranny of these 'giants'.

One day the pair arrive at a small village and they stay at the inn, much to the amusement of the locals. After all, knights haven't been around for three hundred years. Never-the-less, he is humoured and given a room and one for his squire.

Every true knight must have a lady to dedicate his quest to, and the kitchenmaid, who is also the local whore, catches his eye. Yet in his deluded mind he doesn't see a whore but a beautiful princess whom he names Dulcinea del Toboso. He tries to convince her without success that she is indeed a lady of great breeding. She in turn demands he leave her alone unless he is willing to pay for her dubious services.

But he counters with an explanation of his philosophy and of his 'quest' and of his 'impossible Dream'.

He speaks of the human tragedy of submitting to suffering, disease, evil thoughts and deeds. That no man or woman can conceive joy, honour, courage, fortitude and virtue while living out miserable lives. Of a man who, after a torturous life of squalour and suffering, as he dies, asks not why he is dying, but why he had even lived.

He explains that we must dream as high as we are able — to impossible heights. To be prepared to fight against unbeatable odds; to bear unbearable sadness; to go where the brave are frightened to tread; to put right the wrongs which seem unrightable; to be chaste and love unconditionally and from afar; to keep trying when overcome with weariness; to reach up to the highest star. That he will continue to follow this quest, no matter how far or how hopeless; to be willing to fight for all that is right, even if it means marching into hell for a heavenly cause. For he knows if he is steadfast and true to his glorious quest, that when he dies, his heart will be able to rest peacefully. And the world will be better that even one man who is scorned, laughed at and scared, kept striving with his last ounce of courage to reach out to that which seemed unreachable.

This poor overwhelmed young kitchen maid demands that he should remove the clouds from his eyes and see life and her as she really is. That he has shown her the sky but what good is the sky to a creature who does little better than crawl and who men use and forget. That she is just a kitchen maid reeking with sweat. That his gently insanities drive her crazy and that of all the people who abuse and batter her, he is the cruellest of them all. Does he not see how he torments her with his ridiculous kindness as it robs her of anger and gives her despair; abuse she can take and give back again, but tenderness she cannot bear.

At that, she stalks from the room after throwing her dirty cleaning rag in his face. He accepts this as her parting gift, thinking she has accepted him as her knight errant. After all, it is common for ladies to give their knights a pennant to wear into battle. Thus, he enthusiastically ties the rag to the top of his broken lance.

After many adventures his family, who all this time had been most embarrassed with his antics, plan to stop him. They hire some men who will dress up as knights and challenge him to battle. Accepting the challenge from the 'evil knights' he rides out to do battle. But each of his opponents had a shield which was a mirror. As he approached his opponents, he saw for the first time what he really looked like — an old deluded fool trying to act out a dream. The realisation was too much and he went insane (like the rest of us perhaps?). His family took him back home and kept him under close confinement so he wouldn't escape to embarrass them again.

Many years later and after much searching, his old friend and squire and a 'refined' lady finally tracked him down only to find a very old man on his death bed. They managed to get an audience with him in private and the lady tried to get him to remember his former days of glory and righteousness, but no, he could not remember.

She impresses upon him that he was right in believing in his 'quest' and that it had changed her life from a whore to a person with self-respect and dignity. That to dream, to fight/work for righteousness, to bear unbearable sorrows, to show courage, love and virtue and truth was indeed reality. She sings gently to him 'The Impossible Dream' in an attempt to rekindle the memory before he dies. Deep down in long forgotten corners of his mind an ancient memory begins to stir and yes, he at last begins to remember his great days of glory. He raises himself up and joins her in the song and relives his greater days just before he dies. After his death his two loyal friends depart, no doubt to live that way themselves.

The message of Don Quixote came through to me that all the poverty, squalour, disease and despair that he saw around him was not reality. This was only the surface of things and a belief in them made a false appearance of reality. That underneath all this suffering, if men would only look with raised consciousness they would see the true reality. The reality of beauty, love, perfection and joy. In our modern world the murderers, rapists, and drug pushers are as much victims of society that is locked in to a surface appearance of reality as are the victims of their crimes. That war, disease, famine and everything else contrary to human happiness are mere manifestations of a belief in temperol surface appearances of reality, which is unhappiness. That the true reality is hidden from the eyes of most people because their eyes are covered over with the dust of the illusion of suffering.

Perhaps the story of Don Quixote was all about his seeing beyond surface appearances while everyone around him saw a deluded old fool. Yet in reality, he was not insane but was the only one who was really sane and he alone could see the truth. We are taught to think that a person who does not exercise self-control to conform to society's normal behaviour is strange and perhaps insane. Someone who acts differently from what our conditioning tells us is 'correct' behaviour should be perhaps institutionalised.

As each of us is so highly conditioned, none of us has 'Self-control' in the real sense of that word, but is totally controlled by our sub-conscious and programmed conditionings.

The story of Don Quixote can be a very powerful illustration of how all unhappiness is the result of the illusion of conditioning.

CHAPTER 11

THE ART OF RELAXATION

Total relaxation is a state of physical, mental and emotional calm. It is the absence of tension, or stress and high emotionality.

Tension is a conditioned reaction that is needed in order to keep something suppressed. A person with a lot of suppression will have unhealthy levels of tension and stress which burns fine energy continuously.

A certain amount of physical tension is necessary for walking, or doing any movements with muscles. Even sitting in a comfortable chair requires a number of muscles for support. Without this tension we would collapse like a lump of jelly. Unfortunately, most of us tend to use far more effort than is necessary to do things, or even to sit still. We are therefore burning up energy to no purpose. It should be understood that when the body is tense, it is burning energy. When relaxed, it is storing energy. But tension is normal, extreme tension is not. When we feel ill at ease most of the time or feeling nothing at all which means our body awareness is suppressed, we can be sure that we have more stress than is good for us.

Physical reaction to stress is lodged deep in pre-history. Early humankind survived in a harsh world, but along with an elaborate brain, he had the mechanisms of instantaneous, unthinking physical reactions when in danger. Imagine a primitive man resting by a tree after a hunt, digesting his food. Suddenly, he sees a wild predatory carnivore stalking him. Immediately he reacts with a great surge of bodily resources. Into his bloodstream go adrenal secretions that generate strength in the form of sugar and stored fats and flash to his brain and muscles, instantly mobilizing full energy. The heart beat increases stimulating pulse, respiration and blood pressure. Red cells pour from the spleen into the stepped up blood circulation to help the respiratory system take in more oxygen and cast off carbon dioxide. His digestive processes turn off at once so that no energy is diverted from meeting the threat. His coagulation chemistry prepares to resist wounds with quick clotting. All this takes place in a split second as ancestral man fights the attacking beast, or climbs safely up a tree or runs away.

Humankind today reacts in the same chemical way to situations that he thinks are threatening or unpleasant. But today's threat is more likely to be abstract. For example: a cool memo from a superior suggesting that your work is not good enough and therefore you are being moved. Flash go the hormones into the blood and up goes the pulse. But you can neither fight physically nor run. Instead, under forced calm, repressed rage builds up without an adequate target, except yourself. If the threat recedes or is overcome in your own mind, stability returns. But if the attack is prolonged, your defence system gradually wears down and deteriorates.

In today's society the response of 'fight, flight' syndrome as it is called is more likely to be triggered by other people rather than wild beasts or the elements. The negative thoughts and feelings are mostly directed to other people in our lives. While it was once appropriate to react with 'fight, flight' reaction to danger, today, under normal circumstances it is not. This type of reaction leads to open conflict and eventual self-destruction. Therefore we must learn new skills; skills that give us responsibility and control over our thoughts and feelings.

The art of RELAXATION is the basis of any new learning skill that will bring about positive change.

Stress is alright so long as the body is handling it. Handling it means, releasing the tensions as they are gathering. But the over accumulation of stress where the system becomes overloaded through poor diet, faulty physical activity, and the main one, negative thoughts, is destructive. It can make us accident prone, destroy our sense of humour and our common sense; it can ruin beautiful relationships with others; keep us in a constant muddle, making simple tasks seem almost impossible; it can make us feel eternally tired when we could be enjoying life; it is the main cause of insomnia; it reduces our ability to bear pain; and leads to the deterioration of the physical body.

We are not aware of the particular parts of the body that are tense because they are in the form of suppressed negative thoughts. Suppressed negative thoughts were created by us when we withdrew our awareness away from an experience we chose to think was unpleasant. We have probably lived with tension for so long that we are quite unaware of it even forming. But we will certainly be aware of our mind which is anxious. It is here in the mind that causes 99% of our stress, through our habitual way of thinking. If we have an anxious mind then we will have a stressful body.

It must be understood that We are beyond the body and mind, and they are just tools for our use in this creation. If we have trouble relaxing, it is because we have misused these marvellous mechanisms.

We can relax by directing our mind and body to do so. It is that easy. But because we have filled ourselves with so much stress and negative beliefs since we were born, it may appear more difficult than it really is and we may need to clear the system of some of the mental junk, and negative thoughts first. But it is that easy when the system becomes clearer. We can prove this by a practical demonstration.

Right, now try this experiment: Raise your right arm! Open and close your hand a few times! Now wriggle your fingers! All right, did you have any difficulty in doing any of those things? Of course not. Do you know why? Simply because you knew you could do them. You knew without hesitation that your arms and legs, fingers and toes will do as you command them. You have no doubt about it.

The muscles of the body will likewise respond to any mental instructions, as long as we know they will do so. Since we are working on the basis of results first and the theory later, let us experiment further by giving the mind an instruction regarding relaxation.

Read the following paragraph a couple of times, and then put this book to one side and mentally instruct the body and mind to respond fully to the following statements:

"My entire being from head to toe is in a state of perfect relaxation. Tension has been released, removing all physical restrictions, permitting me to experience deep and profound restfulness. I sense a feeling of wholesome well-being as my body accumulates renewed energy."

How do we feel? If we responded to this statement, right now we should not be conscious of any body at all. Complete relaxation means just that. A state is reached where we are almost a mind afloat. Being aware of various parts of the body is an indication that you have not fully relaxed. This is different from not being aware of the body because of stress. Non-feeling of the body because of stress is accompanied by an anxious mind. Non-feeling of the body because of deep relaxation, is an experience of transcending the body and mind to deeper levels of consciousness, having released the stress.

This exercise is even more effective if we can have someone read the relaxation affirmations to us.

We must relax mentally before we can relax physically because our body merely reflects the state of our mind. If the mind is tense, our body will be likewise. An example will illustrate this:

Imagine ourselves standing at the very edge of a very high and steep cliff. Suppose that we lean out to gaze down into the valley far below. Suddenly, we lose our balance and fall over the edge. As we imagine such a thing, do we feel our body growing tense?

Think of a worrying situation in our lives, such as our house burning down, or a loved one having an accident. Doesn't it make us shudder as we hold such a mental picture? Worry is one of the most stress producing activities in the world.

When thinking about eating into a sour lemon, our mouth begins to pucker. Experiments with auto-suggestion have shown that by feeding the mind with a stream of similar thought patterns, either positive or negative, always result in corresponding changes in the body. All these illustrations show that we get physiological reactions from our thoughts. This being true, we can see how impossible it would be to become physically relaxed and stay that way while the mind is tense.

Usually, if there is not too much suppressed tension in the system, making the relaxation affirmations previously given, our mind automatically relaxes, because we are thinking of relaxation. Yet through habitual thinking of our problems, we allow the mind to become tense, preventing us from changing conditioned structures of negative thinking and stopping us from finding solutions to what bothers us. In fact, our situation is likely to create an attitude of avoiding the present moment experience causing more stress, more suppressions and more problems. By mastering relaxation, we gain so much energy that it becomes increasingly easy to handle any problems.

A good affirmation is: 'I control my thoughts, and my mind is dwelling on peaceful, harmonious thoughts.'

The first step towards becoming more relaxed is developing a 'Relaxation Consciousness'. This means being aware of the tension in ourselves, and other people, as much as possible. 'Relaxation Consciousness', is relaxing mentally and physically every time we think of it and we should be aware of it all of the time. It's filling our consciousness with thoughts of relaxation, until we purposefully form a habit pattern of always being relaxed. We should take notice of the way we are walking, working and talking. It is very easy to grip a pen or a tool too hard and so expend more energy than is necessary. Be aware and ask ourselves, 'Am I doing this activity in a tense manner, or am I relaxed?'. By making a habit of thinking about it, we are gradually re-educating ourselves. While eating, while waiting for a bus, while thinking and reading — RELAX!

The face is an area of the body where tension is most readily seen. Check it out now. Is your jaw tightly clenched? Is your forehead creased into a frown of concentration? The habit of frowning can reinforce the tension in the mind. Problems change to interesting challenges when we are relaxed. Screw up your face right now. Hold it for a few seconds and now relax. Do this several times and make sure your face is quite smooth and relaxed before reading on.

Before turning over this page, check your face muscles again. Have they tensed up again? It is important that we become very aware of the face, for keeping it relaxed is a major step in becoming a more relaxed person. A smiling face is a relaxed face.

Tense people face up to new learning situations with all the tension they can muster. 'I'm going to learn to relax if it's the last thing I do,' they will say, as they make a great effort.

THE MOST IMPORTANT POINT ABOUT RELAXATION IS THAT IT IS A LETTING GO OF ALL EFFORT. IT IS NOT SOMETHING YOU DO, BUT RATHER SOMETHING YOU DON'T DO.

If we are observant, we can benefit greatly from the tense people around us. As we go about our daily business, sit in a bus or park, at parties or group gatherings, watch others closely. We won't have to look far to see signs of stress. We will see lines of concentration on foreheads; faces contorted as they talk to one another; women with tense bodies yelling at their children; stiffened bodies when people are criticised or feel threatened are all signs of overloaded suppressed tension. As we observe, make mental checks of our own body to see if we are quite relaxed. Also, observe closely those people around us that appear very relaxed. We will notice that their actions are characterised by ease of movement and poise. They are usually optimistic, cheerful and friendly, even towards strangers.

We all manifest certain degrees of anxiety at some periods in our lives, but those of us who are constantly in a state of tension for no good reason, are likely to age quicker, have re-occuring illnesses, and take all the fun out of life. The business man who suddenly dies in his 40's or early 50's is likely to have been the victim of stress. In this age of high pressure, there has never been a greater need for people to understand and practice the art of RELAXATION.

One of the main benefits of REBIRTHING is RELAXATION. As negative patterns of energy unravel and are cleared, relaxation is something that happens naturally and automatically. We don't need to learn to relax. We simply need to unlearn our negativity and stop making perfection wrong.

RELAXATION IN REBIRTHING

We have discussed the importance of RELAXATION in connection with Rebirthing in Chapter Five, and we need to understand that generally, integration happens more quickly when we are totally relaxed. It is the very key to integrating suppressed material.

We want to emphasize at this point, however, the importance of integrating material at subtler levels of consciousness, rather than allowing the material to become so gross, so intense, that it is uncomfortable. Early Rebirthing was filled with struggle, pain, and unpleasantness. We are into ease, comfort, pleasure and fun, not pain or struggle.

When suppressed material begins to be activated, there is often a strong tendency to resist and struggle against it. Depending on how much suppression and conditioning we have will depend upon how much resistance we put up against the process. At such times we should ask ourselves, 'Do I want to suffer pain and struggle, or do I want pleasure?.

Relaxing into the process is so important, because, commonly the first awareness that we have some suppressed energy is awareness of an area of the body that is tight and not relaxed.

If we resist the process by not relaxing into what is coming up, the energy moving through the body begins to vibrate. This vibration which is perfectly harmless, may frighten us, particularly if we are feeling very unsure of ourselves and the process. What can then happen is we begin to force the exhale in the attempt to get rid of the vibrations, and this forcing can intensify the energy and cause tetany. The experience of intense movement of energy in the body that we may have once insisted was uncomfortable or painful, can teach us a great deal about Bliss and Relaxation. When we become aware of the emotional energy and then let go of the struggle against it, the symptoms disappear and we integrate it into pleasure. Thus we learn that behind all unpleasantness, pain, fear etc., is pleasure and ecstasy. For those of us who have only known the pain and fear, this is good news. Simply by surrendering to any experience, we are allowed to go beyond it and experience the joy of living bliss.

In Leonard Orr and Sondra Ray's book, 'Rebirthing in the New Age', they write:

"Therefore rebirthing is a model for all healing. The elements are as follows: Relax into the symptom so that you can get its message about your mind. Don't be afraid of it. Pain and fear are the effort involved in clinging to a negative thought. Behind all fear and pain is pleasure, which is the physical manifestation of the meta-physical love of God. All pain, all fear and all illness is resisting the pleasure of God's love and wisdom on some level.

Pleasure is natural. All else is unnatural... and ultimately self-destructive. If you don't relax into the pain and go through it to the pleasure that is behind it, life will become too much of an effort and you will love death more than life. Death is loving pain more than you love pleasure."

If we can totally surrender to the process, not only will we avoid the uncomfortable feelings of intense energy, but we will also learn the mastery of the BLISS principle. This principle is the understanding that every experience is highly pleasurable, whether we are aware of it or not.

The key to relaxation and surrender is trust. A trust that we are safe, and that there is no natural force in the universe that will hurt us. A trust that the movement of all energy in the body is good and is there to heal us. A trust that it is our own mind which creates the experiences of what happens in the body, and that we can uncreate any suppressions. A trust that we were born to enjoy and not suffer, and that behind every pain and suffering is our inheritance of perfect ecstasy. A trust in our rebirther, who has him/herself been through all this, and helped numerous other people through the experience and every one not only survived, but benefited greatly from it. If we survived our birth, we will survive our rebirth, and be truly 'born again'.

One last word on relaxation. In my experience, the most effective way to learn to relax is in the regular practice of some sort of centering technique like meditation. One in particular I recommend is 'Trans-cendental Meditation', as taught by the 'TM Relaxation Free Clinics', 17 Horoeka Avenue, Mt Eden, Auckland, New Zealand.

By sending a donation of about $20 00, they will send you a very good correspondence course. Or if you prefer personal instruction and live in Auckland, New Zealand, you may attend one of my meditation courses which run from time to time. The fee is by way of donation or free.

CHAPTER 12

AFFIRMATIONS:
CREATING POSITIVE REALITY

Thoughts are things, incredibly powerful things, although they are very subtle. Nuclear science has revealed that the smaller the particle of matter, the greater the amount of energy it contains. At the smallest possible level, the energy is very subtle. Thoughts are even more subtle and finer than the finest piece of matter in the universe, and so contains powers beyond our wildest dreams. The source of thought is the greatest power of all.

Everything that manifests itself in a person's life is the direct result of his thoughts.

'As a man thinketh so is he.' The thinker is creative with his thoughts. Humans are creative beings and they create with their thoughts. They create their own experience.

If we have the ability to create thoughts and thoughts create circumstances, we therefore, as the master of our own thoughts, have the ability to master circumstances. Since thoughts have such a range and power, this makes us virtually unlimited and the boundaries of what we can do extends to the scope of our thoughts. Our limitations are self imposed and created by our thoughts.

The subconscious means under-conscious, or a consciousness that is beyond our ordinary surface level of awareness. It is made up of thoughts we have had before and is created by thought. In fact, everything in existence was created by thoughts. 'In the beginning was the Word, and the Word was with God, and the Word was God.' The 'Word' is the symbol for sound or vibration and vibration is what this whole creation is made of. Energy is another word for vibration and vibration was created by thoughts. So in the beginning was thought. The beginning was created by thought. The concept of a beginning

73

has to be thought before there can be a beginning.

With this understanding, we realise that our thoughts always produce results. Negative thoughts produce negative results. Positive thoughts always produce positive results. It is as simple as that.

A negative thought is any kind of thinking that is untrue, false or anti-life.

A positive thought is any kind of thinking that is based on truth and is life-supporting.

We have previously discussed the fact that we are always in a state of perfect ecstasy no matter how we are thinking, feeling or acting. Therefore, negative thinking, that is thoughts that induce feelings of fear, anger, pain, frustration, anxiety and every other potential thought and feeling that leads us to decide that something is unpleasant and bad, is certainly negative. This is not saying that negative feelings or thoughts are bad or wrong. It simply means that their basis is false, and because they come from illusion, they make perfect situations wrong by suppression. Suppression is 'turning off' awareness in order to cope. This state of unawareness, which is ignoring something, is ignorance, suffering and anti-life.

We may not be aware of those thoughts that are negative because we have probably lived with them for so long that they are second nature to us by now. But they are not a part of our True Self, which is always in the blissful state of ecstasy.

The suppressions we started at birth and early life experiences, were the result of negative thinking. Negative thinking is the cause of suppression. Since we once decided that an experience was unpleasant (negative), we withdrew our awareness from it and the thought went into suppression and remained in the subconscious until it could be integrated one way or another.

In order to get positive results in our life all the time, we have to convert our negative thought patterns into positive thoughts. We can change our feelings in the same way, since feelings are only structures of thought. A feeling is the physiological reaction to a thought. Feelings are neither positive or negative; they just ARE. Indeed, some are more 'pleasant' than others, but they are only a reaction to what is happening inside our head. It is the thoughts behind feelings that can be negative or positive. Once we understand this and accept it, we are more able to create positive thoughts which will replace or dissolve feelings of a negative nature. Effects in this life are always produced by our previous thinking. The Law of Cause and Effect is based on thought, for all action comes from thought, where reaction comes from action.

We use Rebirthing to integrate suppressions of the past, yet to prevent suppressions reoccurring, we may need to change certain thought patterns; those negative thoughts which caused the suppressions to happen in the first place, and still may be doing so.

Therefore, we use a technique called AFFIRMATIONS. Affirmation is based on the principle of auto-suggestion, and is effective in bringing those unconscious thoughts that are producing effects we don't want, up to the conscious level where we can integrate them.

Our mind is the sum total of our thoughts, and the average person has about 30,000 thoughts a day. Now if some of those thoughts are destructive and negative, and many are because it seems easier to be negative than positive, they become habitual and we become conditioned to think in a particular way. How we think today is based on how we thought yesterday and our past choices. Our conscious mind is governed by our subconscious. Our subconscious in turn is governed by our conditioning and habits of thought. Our conscious mind, which is controlled by the subconscious, is the result of all past thoughts and conditioning, and thus it becomes a vicious circle.

If you doubt this, and many folk on first hearing that they are controlled by their past conditioning do, then consider this: we all dress a certain way, eat certain food, do certain things, talk a certain way, have a certain personality and have mannerisms and traits all peculiar to ourselves. Tomorrow morning, try changing all the things mentioned above, or even just one of them. It is nearly impossible because they are all habits of thought, and those habits are stored in the subconscious, which control our every action.

We view and perceive our world through our minds eye. If we habitually think negatively, we perceive a very dark and gloomy world, as if looking through dark glasses. But the truth is that we and the world are perfect, beautiful and important. If we don't see it this way, then we have been conditioned over a long time to habitually think otherwise. (Remember Don Quixote?) Why we can't see this perfection in ourselves and our world is because we are so full of suppressed negative thinking which has enslaved us. 'Know the truth and it will set you free.'

Affirmations helps to make us free and extends the rebirthing process out into every area of our lives. We need to break habit patterns of thought and instill thoughts of Truth, Harmony, Beauty, Love, Power and Wisdom, which is the reality of life and is what we each are as individuals.

Folk who are full of suppressions and conditionings, who do not equate themselves with truth, love, ecstasy, power and wisdom, who see these things as separate from them, as a power outside themselves, find it hard to accept that to be human is to be these things. But anyone with a little persistence and willingness to realise themselves and find the truth within, can do so very quickly with simple exercises like Rebirthing and Affirmations. The only suffering there is, is denying the truth by the pain and effort that is required to cling to negative thoughts and suppressions.

Affirmations improve and control the quality of our thoughts. It is based on taking responsibility for oneself, and dissolving the suppressions which create illusions of lies and untruths that other people as well as ourselves, have laid on us throughout our entire lives.

Thought purification is the basic principle of any great religion, philosophy or higher teachings. It is impossible to find permanent peace, bliss, love and truth in the conscious mind until we have weeded out the negative thoughts and suppressions from the subconscious. Thoughts like 'I'm a loser', 'I'm no good', 'No one loves me', 'I don't like myself', 'I am weak', and so on. Self-rejection is the manifestation of lies and falseness within us and must be cleared out to make way for the truth.

Negative belief systems are structures of thought and may need changing in order to clear the blockages of unhappiness, allowing the entrance of genuine joy.

As we are human beings and have the ability to create our own experience, we obviously have a great deal of power at our disposal. Yet many of us believe we are weak and vulnerable to possible hostile forces lurking somewhere out there in the Universe. This simply is not true. The Universe is a loving and nurturing existence designed for our personal welfare and development. By believing we are weak, is believing in an untruth, which puts our power outside ourselves. So long as we approach life in this false way, we are resisting the truth of a loving universe and that resistance is experienced by us in pain and anxiety. Our identification with weakness ultimately leads to delaying our eventual development into higher consciousness. Realising that we all have areas in our lives that are weak and need developing, is far different from equating ourselves with weakness. Realising that we *are* in error operates from truth and strength, while believing we *are* the error, comes from lies and weakness.

When we cut ourselves off from truth with negative thinking, we are denying our power, and our experience becomes a lie, and we eventually destroy our physical body through disease, or violent circumstances.

Many folk deny that they think negatively, yet negative things keep happening to them, which they blame on external forces. They have failed to realise the connection between how they think, and the things that happen to them.

We attract to us what we think we are. Therefore, everything that manifests in our lives is of our own making, our own creation. A result of our own thinking.

When people are talking, they are actually expressing affirmations, which are either positive or negative. They are doing it all the time. That is why our method or technique of affirmations is so easy. All we are doing is 're-programming' our subconscious from all the lies, to the truth.

However, some people resist truth and positive affirmations because they fear giving up something that is familiar, even though painful at times. It takes a lot of effort to hang onto destructive thoughts, when statements of truth are being confronted. Negative and positive thoughts cannot exist together anymore than water and fire can exist together. When negative thoughts begin to surface from the subconscious into the gross level of the conscious mind, they demand a lot of energy to hold down, which results in emotions of fear, anger, sadness, anxiety and so on. It is far easier to label this type of self-work as nonsense and crawl back into one's old familiar conditioned, unconscious suffering.

The truth is that each one of us is a beautiful, lovable, peaceful, loving, powerful, blissful centre of TRUTH. Total and complete perfection. This is the truth behind SELF-REALISATION. Only we have covered it up with a lot of conditioned, habitual thinking, ignorance and unawareness. That is why Gurdjieff referred to mankind as being 'asleep'.

Our mind works on the thoughts reaching it and transforms those thoughts into our subjective reality. Our mind is perfect and will do whatever we ask of it. Unfortunately, we have misused this wonderful device. Instead, we have presented to it a stream of negative goals, like worry, fear, anxiety, doubt and negative desires. Remember that negative means anti-life, destructive and untruthful. Whereas positive is truth and life-supporting.

So we describe an AFFIRMATION as a positive truthful thought that we immerse in our consciousness to free us from all that is false.

The repetitive use of AFFIRMATIONS will simultaneously make 'its' impression on the mind and erase the old conditioned thought patterns, producing positive desirable changes in one's life.

It works better if we are able to experience the feeling and the visualisation of the affirmation as we say or write it. We need to be careful in how we word the affirmations because they are very powerful, and results can be startling. As a result of breaking the old structure that controls us, with the new freedom we must be willing to take on the new adventures and challenges that will be our new experience.

However, in my experience, I have found the use of affirmations on their own limited, and any changes that come about are temporary. That is why only about 10 percent of all the people who use affirmation through the numerous 'self-improvement' courses around these days, find lasting benefit. The other 90% experience a rush of profound change, and after, when all the excitement has died down, drift back to their old habitual thinking patterns. Why is this? It is because affirmations are mostly to do with re-programming the conscious mind. Yet it is the subconscious which really needs re-programming, and although affirmations do have a strong influence on the subconscious, I don't believe it reaches far enough. We need to work down into the subconscious, where all our conditionings are, to have truly lasting benefit.

Rebirthing is all about cleaning out the subconscious and integrating all our previous made 'wrongs'.

The use of affirmations in conjunction with a technique like Rebirthing, makes the results of affirmations almost unbelievable. I have witnessed the lasting development of Bliss in too many people not to realise the tremendous power of affirmations while being Rebirthed once a week. No conditioning (ego) can withstand a two-pronged attack, so to speak — one from below with Rebirthing, and one from above through the regular use of affirmations.

Affirmations are a valuable tool towards re-conditioning ourselves positively. But it is still a form of conditioning. This may be a step towards self realisation, but until we free ourselves from the need for the crutch of conditioning in any form, we remain bound within its confines. Being conditioned is a habit and we need to clear all conditioning in order to be fully aware and Self-Realised.

In a state of unawareness we need conditioning to be effective. What is shown here are the problems that arise in us when we are subjected to 'negative' conditioning. Accepting this fact, that an unaware person requires conditioning, we make use of this characteristic by feeding in 'positive' conditioning which we call affirmations, inspirational and success motivational oriented learnings. We have been conditioned into believing that it is better to be conditioned 'positively' rather than 'negatively'. What I'm suggesting is that by clearing ALL conditioning, through Rebirthing, meditation and other centering-type exercises, we go beyond the need to be conditioned at all, and enter the perfect FREEDOM.

Indeed, we will operate more effectively in many areas of our lives by positively conditioning ourselves, but we are still using just another form of conditioning, and therefore can become addicted and dependent upon the conditioning mechanism.

Until we have cleared some of our mental and emotional negativities, most of us will need some form of positive conditioning to bridge the gap between where we are now and to being totally free and happy. Few of us are able to make that jump in consciousness from being negatively conditioned to being free of all conditioning. Therefore, affirmations are the stepping stone towards greater enjoyment, freedom and love, from where we are now.

USING AFFIRMATIONS

1.   Work with at least one every day, and even two or three. The best times are first thing in the morning, and especially whenever you feel discouraged or depressed.

2.   Say or write each affirmation in the first, second, and third person: 'I, (name), totally accept myself. You, (name), totally accept yourself. She/he, (name), totally accepts herself/himself. Using the second and third person works on the conditioning that came from other people. It is important to use your name in the affirmation, and keep the affirmation in the present tense.

3.   Write the affirmation ten to twenty times. Note your responses (thoughts, feelings, considerations, fears or whatever) in a parallel column. This parallel column records all the negative as well as positive feedback or reactions of the mind to the affirmation. It is very important.

eg:

'I..........love myself.'	Like hell I do
'I..........love myself.'	Wish I could
'I..........love myself.'	Maybe
'You............love yourself.'	Why shouldn't I

It is good to change the affirmation to invert your negative response into the affirmations. Keep writing the affirmation and the responses until no more negative responses come up, and you feel comfortable and it is believable. Repeat the process once or twice a day for a week or until the response column goes flat.

4. Sometime during the week, look into a mirror and say the affirmation to yourself aloud. Keep saying it until all facial tension is eliminated and you are able to see yourself with a happy relaxed expression.

5. Record the affirmation on a cassette tape about ten times and play it back to yourself while lying down in a relaxed position. Pause between each recorded affirmation so that you can respond to it and become aware of your responses.

6. Say the affirmation aloud to a friend who is able to observe your body language. Continue until he agrees you are able to say it clearly without contradictory body reactions.

7. If negative thoughts come up during the day, acknowledge them, and accept them as part of your purification or cleansing process. When a person begins this type of self work like Rebirthing, Affirmations and Self-awareness techniques, it is easy to be triggered by simple things in daily life. Negative thoughts can often surface making a person feel sad, angry, anxious and so on. This is because the protective walls of our ego (the barrier that keeps out a hostile world and us trapped inside), are being dissolved, and we can feel a little sensitive and vulnerable. We need only accept that it is part of the process of cleaning out the system. During such times we should focus our full awareness on the feeling and where it is happening in our body. This acknowledgement of any activated material that comes up during the day is very important, as long as we don't become identified, or attached, or morbidly dwell on the thoughts and feelings. At such times, after becoming fully aware of the thought, sensation or feelings, begin saying our affirmation over and over again, until it fills our consciousness and the negativity passes.

The power behind affirmations is our own. This means that we are creating our own reality, as we have always done. Yet now, our new reality is in a positive form rather than in our old familiar habitual negative manner.

LIST OF AFFIRMATIONS

A. Rebirthing Affirmations

1. I survived my birth, therefore I love life more than death, because I chose to survive.
2. I am glad to be out of the womb so I can express myself fully and freely.
3. It is safe for me to breathe fully and freely.
4. I am glad I was born and I have a right to be here.

B. Self-Awareness Affirmations

1. I find it easy to focus on thoughts, feelings and sensations in my body.
2. This is the most important moment in my entire life.
3. My consciousness is expanding as it should.
4. It is safe for me to feel sensations/energy in my body.

C. Ecstasy Affirmations

1. I feel healthy, I feel happy, I feel terrific.
2. I am in a state of Bliss, whether I am aware of it or not.
3. I choose to be happy in every experience.
4. I am a centre of unconditional BLISS.
5. Every experience I once decided was unpleasant is now beautiful and highly pleasurable.
6. Underneath my conditioning, I am a perfect, beautiful, lovable, peaceful, loving, powerful, blissful centre of TRUTH.

D. Relaxation Affirmations

1. It is safe for me to surrender; the more I surrender, the better I feel about being alive.
2. It is easy for me to totally relax and let go.
3. I am totally relaxed; every muscle in my body is in a state of complete surrender.
4. It is safe, easy and highly pleasurable for me to totally surrender to whatever I experience.
5. I truly love to surrender to my energy.

E. Whatever Happens is the Right Happening

1. Whatever happens is the right happening.
2. Everything works perfectly, whatever I do or don't do.
3. Everything is perfect joy.
4. Because everything is perfect, everything I do is perfect.
5. I am always in the right place at the right time, successfully doing the right thing.

F. Life Urge

1. All the cells in my body are daily renewing themselves, therefore I am growing younger.
2. My body is daily expressing more health, energy and strength.
3. The entire universe exists for the purpose of supporting my physical body, and provides a pleasurable place for me to express myself.
4. As long as I continue strengthening my life urges and weakening my death urges, I will go on living in health and youthfulness.

G. Relationship Affirmations

1. Since people treat me the way I treat myself, I am now treating myself fabulously.
2. My relationship with my partner gets more loving, harmonious, happy, honest and healthy every day.
3. All my relationships are now loving, lasting, harmonious.
4. My communication is always clear and productive in my relationship with.........
5. It is safe for me to express myself through sex/love/receiving/ giving etc.
6. Disapproval from.............is okay with me.

H. Specific Positive Affirmations

1. It is easy for me to change.
2. It is safe for me to accept the differences of others.
3. Because I love myself, I no longer need, demand, or expect others to be like me or do things my way.

4. Demands and expectations of others are no longer necessary, because life supplies me with my every need.
5. I forgive myself for............
6. I love myself, therefore I shall enjoy the present moment.
7. I love myself, therefore it is okay for.........to show affection for others.
8. It is safe for me to make decisions.
9. I do things because I really want to.
10. Being treated unfairly is okay with me.
11. I am fully responsible for everything in my experience.
12. I am complete and total within myself.
13. I am my own greatest Hero.
14. Courage. I have an unlimited supply of courage.

I. Self-Love Affirmations

1. I Love myself and I am a lovable person.
2. I am highly pleasing to myself.
3. I am lovable to others and they are lovable to me.
4. It is safe for me to express my love.
5. I am loved and appreciated, whether I am with someone or not.
6. I love every aspect of myself and am a beautiful person.
7. I truly love myself, therefore.....................
8. Because I love myself, I love other people.
9. My heart is full of love and I generate love to all I meet.
10. Today, in every way, I am more loving and kind.
11. Today, my heart is full of love and understanding.
12. There is nothing I have to do or be to love and be loved — I am love.

J. Forgiveness Affirmations

1. I forgive.................... for ....
2. I forgive my parents and others for their ignorant behaviour towards me.
3. I forgive .... for hurting me.
4. I forgive myself for my ignorant reactions towards (parents, spouse, friend etc.)
5. I forgive myself for carrying all that resentment for so long.

K. Self-Responsibility Affirmations

1. I am a self-determined person and I allow others the same right.
2. I have the right to say no to people without losing their love.
3. Disapproval from those I love is okay with me.
4. I am totally in charge of my own life.
5. It is safe to be me, the way I am and the way I want to be.
6. I am responsible for my own feelings.

L. Self-Expression Affirmations

1. I feel safe to express my feelings.
2. Negative attacks from others is my chance to affirm my own self love.
3. It is safe for me to ask questions when I don't understand.
4. I no longer ask permission to do things I know should be done.

M. Health

1. Every day in every way, I feel healthier and stronger.
2. My body is in perfect physical health because I want it to be that way.
3. My body has the power to repair and heal every disease, injury or sickness in the world.
4. My natural state for my body is perfect health, and that is how my body will be.

N. Spiritual Affirmations

1. The entire universe was created for my benefit.
2. My connection with Infinite Intelligence enables me to.....
3. As part of the Absolute (God), I have the ability to.......
4. Every day in every way I am becoming more Christ/Buddha/Krishna etc. conscious.
5. I am One with God and therefore I am unlimited.

O. General Enrichment Affirmations

1. Health and happiness is my natural state.

2. Where I am, what I'm doing right now, is meant to be and I'm loving every moment of it.
3. My life is wonderful and it is getting better all the time.
4. Today, positive, beautiful and loving things are going to happen to me and everyone I meet.
5. Today, I happily accept and am thankful to everything in my life.
6. The universe loves, supports and protects me.
7. I now receive assistance and co-operation from people.
8. I daily make valuable contributions to the growth of myself, of others and of humanity.
9. Everything I give is returned to me 100 fold.
10. Life rewards me with abundance.
11. I deserve to be wealthy.
12. My income now exceeds my expenses.

These are just a sprinkling of affirmations you can use of the many thousands that you can think up for yourself. As your Rebirthing sessions develop, certain affirmations pertaining to you personally will be more effective. Your Rebirther will help you create new affirmations best suited to you.

PART TWO

UNRAVELLING OUR PERSONAL LAW

CHAPTER 13

PERSONAL LAW

Most philosophies and followings in the world focus on the negative traits that humankind seem to suffer from. This enables each person to realise the areas in their lives they need to clean up.

Gurdjieff taught that there are twelve problem areas of which each person has at least one negtative area predominant. Each person has a negative chief feature which is part of his personality and which causes him to create suffering for himself.

In Rebirthing we have found that as the subconscious mind becomes conscious, it reveals a lot of memories relating to causes of why we adopted certain negative personality traits. This knowledge enables us to work at the very origin of why, how and who we are.

The study of our personal law reveals the original reason why we decided that certain experiences were bad, unpleasant and so on. Once having divided up our experiences into good and bad, pleasant and unpleasant, etc., our personality becomes dominated by negative ideas that manifest themselves as 'self-sabotaging' actions. These 'self-sabotaging' acts, which Leonard Orr referred to as 'specific negatives', dominate and control our flow of consciousness from the subconscious. These 'self-sabotaging' actions are the result of influences and conditionings from early life experiences, such as parents, learnings, environment and how we decided to respond to them. If we decide that a certain experience was bad, then we will always thereafter try to avoid similiar experiences, or suppress them when we are confronted by them. This creates a conditioned reaction to certain 'unpleasant experiences', which is to try and avoid or hate certain conditions because we have decided they are bad. The nett result is we only 'hurt' ourselves, in contrast to what the universe is trying to teach us — to live effectively, happily and lovingly.

For example, if I see my partner showing affection to some other person, I may believe that she or he is preferring that person to me. What I've done is decided that my partner's action is wrong and become upset with jealousy. If I have been conditioned into believing that my partner should show affection only to me, then I will upset myself when my conditioning is exposed to situations I believe to be wrong. Thus, my feelings become an automatic reflex action of jealousy. With this strong emotion, I am likely to react to my partner with strong resentment and even violent action. This I call 'self-sabotage', because I have destroyed my surface happiness, due to something happening outside myself.

The dominant controlling factor in our lives is our programmed conditioned reactions. A conditioned reaction is when our responses are automatic, without much thought. These conditioned responses are buried in our subconscious and are related to the past, so our present moment consciousness is completely controlled, unknowingly, by our past conditioning. Once a negative idea establishes itself as a belief and is repeated enough times, it becomes a conditioned reaction and we have little control over it thereafter.

How can we break free from our past conditioning and self-sabotage actions? It is not easy, as every person who has tried to give up an old habit like drinking, smoking and drug abuse and so on, has found out. It is not easy because we are attached to the idea that it is hard. In reality we need only stop making things wrong, and anyone can do that if they dare. It is as easy as we like to make it.

After about four or five Rebirthing sessions, a lot of 'stuff' begins to clear away and we get in touch with our *Personal Law.*

Personal Law is the root cause of why we have adopted a certain negative personality trait which keeps us running frantically in circles trying to find love, peace and prosperity. Knowing what our own personal law is, is a major key in the jig-saw puzzle of life and gives us the understanding of negative personality conditioning and how to deal with it.

Personal Law is based upon the premise that we are always right. We have a belief structure that we have built over the years of how it all is — our belief in what is true and what is wrong.

If we have developed a belief structure based upon the dualities of right and wrong, good and bad, joy and fear etc., then we will have built a strong support for 'suffering'.

The duality trip is playing a losing game. When perceiving certain experiences as bad, our belief system will be negative (anti-life) and could include:

- People frighten me.
- Men dominate me.
- Things in the universe can hurt me (people, bacteria, natural disasters, etc.)
- I need people to give me what I need.
- I need approval to support my points of view.
- I need security to survive.
- I may make a wrong decision.
- I don't deserve love/money/comfort.
- I must get angry to get people to do what I want.
- I am a sinner.
- I should feel guilty when I make a mistake.
- I should worry about my loved ones.
- I can't get enough love/money/joy.
- There is value in struggle and difficulty.

This list could go on forever and each message is reinforcing a belief system which is a pack of lies. When we came out of the womb, we decided in an instant that this was a hostile place to be, and we have supported that notion ever since. When our parents told us we were no good we believed them. When we got bashed up at school, we concluded that other people could exert control over us and hurt us.

We have been acting this way ever since without questioning the truth if these beliefs. After all, we see the evidence of these conclusions every day in our lives, because we create them. The more evidence we need to justify a belief about the above list, the bigger the lie. For example, if we were brought up in a poor family, we may have been told that people with lots of money are bad in some way. We take on our parents belief that rich people are bad and therefore, to feel safe, we will always subconsciously stop ourselves from ever having enough money. The idea that we might be wrong never occurs to us. If it did, we would quickly dismiss it, because the thought that we have been supporting a lie for 20 odd years or more, offends and threatens our belief structure of already knowing what is right.

To survive in this so called 'brutal' world, based upon our misconceptions, we play a number of power games in an attempt to get our needs met.

MANIPULATION — Making others feel bad so they will do what we want.

CONDITIONAL GIVING — So others will give us something back.

SELF-RIGHTEOUSNESS — Trying to make others like us.

BLAMING OTHERS — The cause of our problems and anxious feelings.

DEMANDING — Expecting others to fulfil our needs.

DEPENDENCY — Being dominated in order to get security.

SELF-PITY — Which is saying 'don't hurt me because I'm already hurting myself.

They are all games and the trouble is there are no winners.

Negative belief structures have been largely formed from the opinions of other people. We once accepted the opinion of someone who said something was bad, or we were bad, and we have continued believing it ever since. Worse, we continue to believe in the mere opinions of others and never wake up to our own opinions.

We are Divine Beings, therefore sickness, unhappiness, anxiety, fear, etc. are foreign and unnatural to us, yet we continue to create what we believe.

Love, truth, joy, abundance and perfection is what WE are and anything contrary to these is a lie.

So why aren't we happy? Because we support the notion that a lack of whatever we are short of, and pain is necessary for life. What *bloody nonsense*. We all instinctively know this to be untrue, so why are we acting as if it is true? BECAUSE WE DON'T LIKE TO BE WRONG. To break this negative belief system we need to dare to believe that we just might be wrong. We need to dare to believe that the things we currently hold as true may be a lie.

How do we unravel those beliefs which are untrue, and therefore causing unhappiness in our lives, from those that are really true?

The first thing we need to do is give up the notion that unhappiness is true and that fear, anger, jealousy, sadness, anxiety, etc. are simply misinterpretations of the truth. If we believe any negative emotion is true, then we buy into the illusion of the unreal. Reality is real; illusion is false and therefore non-existent. The negative emotions themselves are real, because they are physical manifestations, but their cause is false and therefore non-existent.

We start to give up the ego when we give up the illusion that we must always be right. But more importantly, we need to become aware of the illusions — the negative beliefs that make our experience wrong. After all, it is better to be wrong and happy than always right and miserable.

The following exercises are designed to discover our insanity (lies) which supports belief systems of untruth. Complete each of the following sentences. Do not spend too much time on any one and write down whatever occurs. The more open we are with our answers, the closer we will come to our basic limiting beliefs.

Exercise 1.
1. I don't believe I can . . . .
2. People have always told me I'm . . . .
3. People have always told me I can't . . . .
4. I always feel bad when I . . . .
5. I always feel ill when I . . . .
6. I believe I'm inadequate when . . . .
7. I hate myself when . . . .
8. I am not worthy of receiving . . . .
9. When in the company of others, its hardest for me to . . . .
10. I don't seem to get enough of . . . .
11. I am most afraid to . . . .
12. My biggest concern about money is . . . .
13. My biggest fear about sex is . . . .
14. Its hard to forgive myself for . . . .
15. If only I could . . . .

Three of my greatest fears are:
1. . . . .
2. . . . .
3. . . . .

Three of my greatest joys are:
1. . . . .
2. . . . .
3. . . . .

Three of my main life goals and purposes are:
1. . . . .
2. . . . .
3. . . . .

Exercise 2

If I dared to Believe . . . . (what I want to be/do/orhave) . . . .

However, since I believe . . . . (current situation) . . . .

I can't . . . . (achieve, change, get what I want) . . . .

Because . . . . (negative belief) . . . .

Example:

If I dared to believe *I could be rich*; however, since I believe *I'm poor* I can't *become rich* because *I don't believe I deserve it.*

Basic Limiting Beliefs which are revealed for me from the above questions and exercise are:

1. . . . .

2. . . . .

3. . . . .

Exercise 3

DARE TO BE MISTAKEN

1. What if I was mistaken about. . . . . (negative belief) . . . . ?

2. What would happen if I totally reversed my belief about . . . . . ?

. . . .

3. What is stopping me . . . . (another negative belief) . . . . ?

4. I . . . . (affirmation for what I want to happen) . . . .

Repeat this exercise again on another piece of paper at the end of this chapter.

These exercises demonstrate our negative belief patterns in relation to our Personal Law.

Personal Law can be divided up into five laws which are consciousness factors that cause unhappiness and are related to things that happen to us and our response to them.

1. The Birth Trauma.
2. The Subconscious Death Urge.
3. Other Life-times.
4. Authority Disapproval Syndrome.
5. Self-Sabotage Conditioning.

CHAPTER 14

THE BIRTH TRAUMA

The birth trauma relates to the impressions we formed about the world when we were born and even before, which were either positive or negative. This was the beginning of 'The world is against me'; 'This new environment is painful and uncomfortable'; 'Life is a struggle'; 'I can't get enough (air, love etc.)'.

I discussed the birth trauma in the first chapter. So briefly — it is often the beginning of suppressing material we decided was unpleasant.

The birth trauma is one of the reasons most people find it hard to get out of bed in the morning and that the bed simulates the womb experience prior to being born. Hot showers and baths also stimulate this pre-birth experience.

Many difficulties in some people's lives can be traced back to the birth trauma, particularly physical discomfort and pain. They never really experience lasting physical comfort. It is either too hot, too cold, too wet, too dry, too windy, too etc., etc. Something is always wrong with their immediate environment which gives them discomfort.

If our conclusion about birth experience was negative, we have carried around with us ever since, the feeling that this world is not a pleasant place to be in.

So we build walls around us to protect us from a hostile world, because everything outside the womb is a potential danger. We are frightened to try anything daring or new because we tell ourselves that we will get hurt.

We spend most of our waking hours protecting ourselves, so that by the end of the day, we have tired ourselves out with the stress of mere survival and cannot wait to go to bed (back to the womb.) We turn off the light, crawl under the blankets and raise our body temperature, all of which simulate the womb experience — darkness, enclosure and warmth. The thought of getting out of bed in the morning is unpleasant because subconsciously we remember the trauma of leaving the womb.

We spend well over one-third of our lives in bed and for many of us it represents our retreat from a 'brutal' and 'hostile' universe. But the universe was created for our benefit and is here to support and love us. By opening ourselves up to the gentle compassionate vibration of creation, we can see that outside our mental walled-in fortress, a beautiful world full of beautiful people await us to share in the joy and celebration of life.

CLAUSTROPHOBIA

Claustrophobia is an aversion to enclosed places which could be closely related to the birth trauma. There is a strong suggestion that the subconscious mind remembers the birth and associates all confined spaces with the agony of the birth trauma. People who suffer from claustrophobia experience feelings of panic and of being trapped, which only subsides when they are removed from the confined area. What I'm suggesting is that when they are confined, the subconscious mind believes that a terrible agony will follow the confinement, as was the case of being in the womb and then experiencing an extremely uncomfortable birth. When they came out of the womb and decided the experience of birth was so terrible they concluded that any future confined space experiences would result in a repeat of the birth agony. Thus every time they are confined in a small area, the subconscious mind triggers an unconscious memory with anticipation of the forthcoming pain. When the birth trauma is integrated through Rebirthing, claustrophobia may very well be cured.

Many habits of negative thinking can be traced back to our birth experience. If we decided that it was a painful and horrible experience, then we probably created the belief that the universe and many things in it are out to hurt us; that it is an unsafe universe. No doubt, the belief in a 'Devil', or a punishing God was created as a result of these negative impressions at birth. But the truth is, that there is nothing unsafe or bad in the universe.

The technique of Rebirthing enables us to go back and integrate the birth trauma as an experience of being born into ecstasy.

CHAPTER 15

THE SUBCONSCIOUS DEATH URGE

The birth trauma is probably what began our habit of suppressing difficult life experiences. From this, we perpetuate negative conditions in our life, which control how we think, feel and act. This negative energy could be described as a 'death urge'.

When we refuse to accept some part of our life experience and suppress it, we in fact suppress a portion of our life urge. This can result in one small negative thought colouring our whole attitude, so that we see everything negatively and view life and the universe as full of suffering. This may be a subconscious wish to die and escape from a hostile world.

It manifests itself subtley in people being accident prone, suffering numerous illnesses or poor health, and a belief in any structure of ideas promoting violence and destruction. Most 'liberating freedom fighters' and terrorists have a lot of their life urge suppressed and are primarily motivated by a death urge. Their acts of terror against people and property act as a focal point for their own non self-acceptance, and their suicide missions and high death-risk operations are the expression of their wish to die while bathed in so-called glory.

However, even though we are not trying to kill others or ourselves, just about all of us do have a subconscious death urge to some degree. This urge comes to the surface every time we feel we want to destroy something (or someone), feel angry, or want to avoid or escape from some difficulty in our lives.

The desire to 'end it all' and commit suicide comes when our life urge is so suppressed that our subconscious death urge becomes fully conscious, and is triggered by our refusal to accept a part of our life situation, and in our thinking that something is just too terrible to face. Few of us would carry out this 'end it all' death urge, but most of us are capable of experiencing it when we deny the truth that all is perfect joy and put ourselves into a difficult situation which evokes the fear of a terrible outcome.

While most of us are not faced with such extremes in our everyday life, we do manifest the subconscious death urge in subtle ways, such as always being the victim of accidents, from cutting ourself whilst chopping the vegetables, to someone *else* smashing into our car. Accident-prone people have a fair amount of suppressed life urge in them, which can manifest itself in a series of incidents apparently occurring consecutively within a certain time-span.

The reason for this chain of events is that the death urge is particularly strong during such times and then it sinks back into deeper consciousness until the person has another round of non-acceptance in their life. The point is, accidents don't just happen. They are always caused, but only by the people who feel their effects, and they are caused by not taking responsibility for some aspects of one's life.

Since our thoughts are creative we can subconsciously create situations where accidents are actually 'caused' by other prople. We may avoid an aspect of our life by not accepting it and a certain thought can manifest itself by creating a situation which causes some other person, also loaded with a subconscious death urge, to involve us in 'his accident', so we become the victim of someone else's accident. But this is not true, because we are our own victim. It is simply not possible to have an accident or be a victim of someone else's accident if we have no suppressed life urge. The death urge in us will cause us to subconsciously set ourselves up, or to enter a chain of events involving other people (also with a death urge) to create accidents.

Every negative experience like having our house burned down, is related to the unconscious death urge. We must never forget that we are creative beings and create our own reality. Until we accept that fact, we will avoid responsibility for our own life and everything that happens to us, inhibiting our growth into higher consciousness. If we arrive home and find our house burgled it has nothing to do with the burglar, but a self rejecting subconscious negative thought from our past. This understanding stops us from blaming all exterior conditions and puts the responsibility exactly where it belongs — WITH US. Negative as well as positive events are always created by the person who feels the effects. This is the true meaning of the law of cause and effect or karma.

Poor health and illness again are the subtle manifestations of suppressed life urge. Something in our psyche is telling us that we are not worthy of good health and feelings of well-being. And so we contract some illness like a cold, or even something more serious, in order to be obedient to our programmed subconscious death urge. The symptoms of disease are only an outer effect. The cause is always the result of negative thought patterns. For every effect there is a thought that precedes and maintains it. Our habitual thought patterns create our every experience.

The 'germ theory' is an avoidance of self-responsibility. Certainly, with many diseases there is always the evidence of bacteria, which science believes is the cause of the disease. But the true underlying cause has and always will be erroneous thoughts and fears that things in the universe can hurt and kill us. Very few people have ever sat down and questioned their beliefs about why things happen to them. Its much easier to avoid responsibility and explain away our illnesses with 'I caught a cold from so and so'; 'Pressure from my work gave me a heart attack'; and it never occurs to anyone that cancer is caused by the patients themselves, through harbouring long standing resentment 'eating away at them'. Burns are always created by deep seated anger. Asthma is caused by feeling stifled and smothered. Arthritis is caused by bitterness, hatred and feeling unloved. Eye and ear ailments are related to refusing to see and hear certain truths. Alcoholism is caused by guilt and self hate. Menstrual problems are caused by rejecting one's femininity, with guilt, fear and a belief that the genitals are sinful or dirty. And so it is with every physical disease which first begins with a mental disease.

The word disease means dis-ease — a loss of ease and natural harmony. All disharmony is caused by negative thoughts, and the evidence of bacteria, virus, growths, etc. are only the effect. However, it must always be remembered that the reason we are alive is because our life urge is stronger than our death urge. No matter how rotten, how ill, how depressed, or how violent we may feel, our life urge is always stronger and remains that way, right up to the point when we actually 'drop our body'.

Life insurance is another method for avoiding self responsibility. With it we are in fact planning our own death. Life insurance is actually death insurance; sickness and accident insurance is born from the fear of a hostile universe.

This death urge probably began for most of us because of the birth trauma. However, it can start at any time we begin to suppress anything, because suppression is the cause of the subconscious death urge. Nevertheless, Rebirthing will integrate it, promoting fewer accidents, better health and longer life. When we begin to accept full responsibility for our own life and everything that is happening in it, we begin to become the Master or Mistress of ourselves and the subtle forces influencing and surrounding us. The Absolute within us begins to be awakened.

A good affirmation to use is:

'I love life and life loves me.'

'My life urge is free, vibrant and strong.'

Leonard Orr and Sondra Ray in their book 'Rebirthing in the New Age' talk about the subconscious death urge from another approach which I find interesting and I quote:

"The unconscious death urge is the belief that death is inevitable. The habit people have to affirming the power of death causes not only death, but also many illnesses and states of weakness leading to death. Scientists now suspect that the reason death has been so popular for so many centuries is simply because no-one ever questioned it. Some scientists are now declaring that man can banish death altogether from his experience. In reaching this conclusion they are merely re-affirming what the spiritual masters have been trying to teach us for thousands of years: There is an alternative to physical death and that is physical immortality. (Or not dropping your body). The alternative to ageing is youthing..."

Leonard and Sondra both go on to add some very interesting examples and points which reinforce their philosophy of physical immortality. Points like: developing a permanent health consciousness; that the human body which contains the highest expression of Infinite Intelligence should last as long as the rest of the physical universe made of the same substance; that as thoughts are creative, what the mind thinks, it produces, and that it can produce physical immortality if we want it; that the cells in our body are always renewing themselves with new cells, and that the only thing that ages is our mind which creates older cells, in correspondence with the beliefs programmed into it, with a death wish mentality; that all death is suicide; that it takes more effort to destroy the physical body than to preserve it which means that optimum health and long life is more natural, and numerous other examples.

Another point they make:

"Even if death is inevitable, it won't hurt you to believe in Physical Immortality. It is the safest belief there is. If you are going to die anyway, the idea of Physical Immortality won't make a difference, so you might as well believe in it; it might have the practical benefits of making you feel healthy and wonderful while you are here. When you give up your mortal mentality, you will feel a wonderful difference."

Whether we choose to believe or disbelieve in Physical Immortality is not an issue in this book, but I suggest its contemplation is an excellent mental exercise, and has value in coming to grips with the subconscious death urge at a conscious level.

What is an issue in this book, is finding lasting happiness, love and peace in the here and now experience.

Whether Physical Immortality, karma, life hereafter, or any other belief is true or not is not that important in relation to Rebirthing. The point is, Rebirthing is a wonderful technique and not a philosophy or religion. Rebirthing works and that is sufficient.

Any belief is just another form of conditioning. Self-Realisation is about cleaning out ALL conditionings and self limiting structures of thought, especially a belief in anything that is false which creates suppression of our life urge.

CHAPTER 16

OTHER LIFE-TIMES

Those of us who believe in having had other lives find it interesting as to why we can't remember them, which is of course a strong argument for those who don't believe in other life times.

Locked in our subconscious is the memory of every experience we have ever had as a human being, in this life and all others. The reason we can't remember them is because they are subconscious and not conscious. This explains why through hypnosis, auto-suggestion and regression type techniques, people can again remember things that happened in some other life time. We have already discussed why we have a subconscious and that our habit of suppressing may have begun a very long time ago and was probably passed on down the line to our present life, from which we are perpetuating the habit.

What we are today is the sum total of every single experience we have ever had. Although our personality and character is largely due to the early experiences of this life time, there is an under-current influence from other life times (past and future). Yes, future life times, because outside of this plane of existence where we are now, there is no time as we know it. There is Timelessness. This goes to show that this present life is the most important we have ever lived, or ever will. If it wasn't, then we would be living that one *now* instead of this one. Remember that *Eternal Now?* By living in the present moment, we over-ride all influences from other life times. Until we begin to live in the present moment we remain bound in our conditioning from the past.

Any flaw in our character or personality which is not caused by any conditioning in this life time could be an influence of something that happened in some other life time.

For those of us who don't believe in reincarnation, my suggestion is not to accept openly what is written here, nor reject it out of hand. Just let these ideas sit in our minds and let life either confirm or deny the question of other life times, which it will in time. That I guarantee.

CHAPTER 17

THE AUTHORITY DISAPPROVAL SYNDROME

The authority disapproval syndrome is a major cause of fear and negative, addictive, conditional programming. It manifests as a fear of people, particularly those that we allow to have a margin of control over our lives: people that have authority over us. This fear generates a desire to constantly please and avoid at all costs being disapproved of by anyone.

This authority disapproval syndrome began for those of us that have it as a result of the negative influence from our parents. In order to get us to 'behave properly' our parents used a technique of discipline called manipulation. Manipulation means making us feel bad, naughty, evil or wrong through punishment, either physically or verbally, in the form of disapproval.

As we are Divine Beings when we are born and totally self-approving, disapproval from our parents in any form was confusing to us. Our natural response was to resist such inconsistencies, but we quickly learned that we couldn't win, and so formed the impression that we were bad in some way. After all, the most important person in our life, our mother, when displaying disapproval of us, even if she was teaching us how to sit on a potty, confused our sense of self-worth. As young children we resented this disapproval, but being unable to assert ourselves and win, learned to suppress our true feelings. Because the love we received was conditional, based on 'proper' behaviour, we probably have spent the rest of our lives resenting our parents or trying to please them in order to win their love and approval.

Our parents used manipulation on us, not to hurt or teach us to hate ourselves (which is often the result), but because they were the product also of manipulating parents. Our grandparents were also the product of this form of behaviour, which has been passed on down from generation to generation, until our parents came along.

This pressure upon our parents as children to constantly conform to their parents demands for 'correct' behaviour and perform in such ways as to win approval, was later transferred to teachers, employers, authority figures, spouse and society as a whole. They probably felt limited and frustrated until they had their own children, and that is when we joined the cycle. Here was a defenceless child (us), to mould and manipulate into giving them affection and to release their pent-up frustrations of parental hostilities against, whenever we refused to conform.

It is common for parents to take the frustrations and hostilities they harbour towards their parents out on their children. By attempting to discipline us through disapproval, our parents were teaching us to question our self-worth. But initially, we probably resisted quite fiercely, by doing things intentionally the way we knew to be opposite to what our parents wanted from us. As we had so little control over anything, the chance to resist was strong in us. So feeding, potty training, bedtime, and learning new things were areas we could gain a margin of control.

The constant conditioning that we were naughty in some mysterious way, brought us to the conclusion that there was something wrong with us, and therefore we must disapprove of ourselves. So, our resistance eventually became less and less as our spirit began to break and we surrendered our trust in our perfect inner nature, for exterior control. We decided to do as we were told. We have been doing what we have been told ever since, having buried our natural creativity and initiative. The punishment for not following instructions was a fate worse than death. Authority disapproval could come to us in physical beatings, being ignored (silent treatment), verbal abuse, or even a fierce glance in our direction. Our reaction to any of these was to experience feelings of total fear, guilt and depression. Our reaction was so complete in gut twisting, sweat producing, immobilising fear, that we began to avoid any situation that might involve any form of disapproval from anyone. Thus, a great deal of our energy and time was spent seeking approval from everyone we met, to the point that approval became an addiction, an absolute need.

There is nothing wrong in receiving approval. Compliments and applause always feel good, but when it becomes a *need* rather than a *want*, we have an addiction and are easy victims of manipulation by other people. The extent to which we need approval, measures how much we can be manipulated through feelings of guilt, fear, and worry, when others refuse to give us approval.

The need for approval is based on the assumption that our worth is measured by what others think of us. Our own opinion does not count. Instead, the opinions of others, especially those in authority, are more important. Therefore we have every reason to feel unworthy, depressed, guilty or fearful when their approval is withheld. Approval-needing behaviour is a form of self-rejection, because our parents used rejecting behaviour on us, and so taught us to reject ourselves.

If the need for approval is based on the measure of what others think of us, the whole authority disapproval syndrome is based on the single factor that we must not *trust ourselves.* The lack of self-trust or self-confidence is at the back of all approval-needing behaviour.

Because we were taught at an early age not to trust ourselves, we spend the rest of our lives searching for people to give us instructions. Instead of learning to think for ourselves, we would rather find someone who will think for us. Besides, there is just too much risk involved in thinking and doing for oneself, because if we do the wrong thing, we may get a dose of disapproval — to be avoided at all costs.

When we were old enough and left home, we went looking for someone to tell us what to do. We may have found the parent substitute in an employer, a friend or a spouse. We needed someone to make all our decisions, plan our life, solve our problems and give us approval. And in the case of our spouses, they don't do it! Our mates don't do it because they are also expecting the same from us. Falling in love and entering a relationship is all about finding the right person, and that person in the authority disapproval syndrome means a hope that we have found a parental substitute.

The behaviour of children, when they grow up, in financial and particularly marital relationships, resembles that of their parents' behaviour, and is so strikingly the same that it seems that they inherit a portion of the parents' subconscious mind as well as their bodies. It is not surprising when we realise that we learn from our models — our parents. Their need for approval was so strong that it naturally became our addiction also.

While we may not recall consciously all of our approval-seeking signals that came to us as a child, it was at an early age that the authority disapproval syndrome became a controlling factor in our lives.

Our parents' intentions towards us were not malicious or designed to hurt us. They were motivated, as far as they were consciously aware, to protect us from hurting ourselves and for reasons of health. And while many lessons were important for our health and safety we also learned to keep in line and conduct proper behaviour; behaviour that would win their approval. Thus, approval which should have been given freely was used to bestow reward for proper conduct, and disapproval used as a weapon of punishment. This bred a self-critical concept, and therefore we began to confuse our own self-worth with other people's approval. We learned that if we are disapproved of, then we should also disapprove of ourselves — a concept of self-rejection and self non-acceptance.

Becoming aware of the authority disapproval syndrome in our lives enables us to break the cycle with our children, and makes us aware of our constant need for approval, which begins to dissolve it. When we are disapproving of someone, then we are in our 'critical parent state' and replaying our parents' old tape. Rather, we can either be rebirthed to integrate the suppressed parental hostility, or alternatively we can express how we feel towards our parents and help get it out. Either way will enable us to love them more.

CHAPTER 18

SELF-SABOTAGE CONDITIONING

The word 'sabotage' means to wilfully do damage to the wheels of industry, by workers on bad terms with their employer.

Self-sabotage in the context that is being used here, means to unconsciously hurt ourselves, to destroy aspects of our lives that lead to our happiness.

Our lives run according to habit patterns often based upon a number of beliefs which have become entrenched as conditioned reactions. For example, if I have a lot of self rejection, I will find it hard to believe that anyone else can love me. If, upon entering a relationship with a person who appears to love me, my thinking will probably go like this: 'Just wait until they really get to know me, then they are bound to lose interest in me. Therefore, I will break off the relationship first, before they do.'

THIS IS SELF-SABOTAGE

A person wants to partake in a sporting activity, or learn a new exciting skill; something that person has always wanted to do. As the time approaches to begin, something always intrudes: a business meeting, a family fight, sprained ankle, or the person just cannot find the time. Always putting things off which would lead to enjoyment and fulfilment.

THIS IS SELF-SABOTAGE.

Self-sabotage conditionings are the negative thoughts, beliefs and subconscious programming that control how we think, feel and act.

Most people think that they are in control of themselves, but not so, as 99% of us have a highly programmed conditioned personality which prevents us from living effectively. We have lived with it for so long now, that it has made us quite predictable and mechanical.

Our self-sabotage conditioning probably began with the birth trauma and was reinforced by the Authority Disapproval Syndrome, but we may have reinforced them, perpetuated them and created many new ones.

The first four personal laws (Birth Trauma, Death Urge, Other Life-times and the Authority Disapproval Syndrome) are related to our response to outside influences. As a baby and young child, we were pretty vulnerable. But as an adult we have continued to respond to outside influences, particularly other people, in the same negative way. Our perception has been one of defending ourselves against a hostile universe.

Self-sabotage conditioning is mainly to do with relationships, and particularly the relationship we have with ourselves. We are all familiar with the people we have a relationship with, but how many of us are really familiar with ourselves? If we are honest, very few of us will be familiar with the Self, or our relationship with ourselves.

The single most important relationship we have is with oneself, and all others are dependent upon that one. We cannot have an effective relationship at any level (mental, physical, emotional or spiritual), and at the same time have a 'wrong' relationship with our Self. We must clean up how we relate to our Self before any other relationship will respond.

It is difficult to examine what relationship we have with ourselves, just by looking at ourselves, until we have developed higher consciousness.

This is because we cannot see past our programmed conditioning. However, we can examine our relationship with our self by scrutinising the kind of relationships we have with others, and the way they treat us. We form relationships with people who will treat us the way our subconscious programmed conditioning says we should be treated. The way we have been conditioned, (as children or unaware adults), either by our parents, teachers or even ourselves, is the way we believe we ought to be treated (or mistreated). We have virtually no control over how these relationships run their course and they can tell us a lot about the way we feel about ourselves. The way other people treat us is exactly the same way we treat ourselves. The way this works we will discuss later on.

The basic types of relationships that we form are with:

1. Our Self;
2. Truth, or Absolute, or God, or whatever we call our Source;
3. Our parents;
4. Our life partner;
5. Our children;
6. Friends, acquaintances and groups.

When we tidy up the relationships we have with our Self, we tidy up every other relationship in our lives automatically. If we are having trouble in one relationship, for instance our marriage, it is a total waste of time trying to repair any damage there while neglecting the necessary work on oneself. The reason we are having trouble in any area is because we are not right with our Self.

Self-sabotage conditioning is a self-inflicted conditioning, because we have been denying the truth that we are beautiful, lovable, worthy and important.

As we go through this part of the book, we will see where we have been sabotaging ourselves unconsciously, and understand that all self-sabotage conditioning is the result of not accepting ourselves unconditionally. Here are a few common Specific Negatives.

1. SELF-REJECTION

"I am not good enough", "It never works," "People don't like me", "I hate myself", "I'm bad", etc.

Self-rejection is a behaviour that denies the truth within us, with lies and self put-downs. We may be more accepting to other people's good points, but we ignore our own. It boils down to the fact that we just don't love ourselves. People seem to think that loving themselves is egotistical and wrong, yet their ability to love others is based on how much love they have for themselves.

Most of us seem to connect our self worth with:

(a) the feelings and thoughts we have about ourselves;
(b) our behaviour;
(c) the behaviour of others towards us.

The truth is, our self-worth is totally unrelated to our negative self-assessments, our behaviour, and other people's behaviour towards us. We are beautiful, lovable, worthy and important, regardless of how we think or 'feel' about ourselves, our behaviour or the behaviour of others towards us. To think otherwise will cause us to sabotage every chance we have of happiness and love.

2. LIMITING SELF LABELS PREVENTING GROWTH

These are the negative beliefs we have about ourselves, a mental blueprint of the sort of person we imagine ourselves to be. "I'm shy", "I'm clumsy", "I'm too fat, skinny, short, tall etc.". "I'm poor at spelling, maths, reading etc.", "I'm to old to change", "I'm bad tempered", "I can't do that", "I can't remember things", etc.

Labels enable us to:

- justify staying as we are;
- justify poor performance;
- avoid taking risks;
- explain behaviour we dislike in ourselves;
- apply a useful tool in manipulating others.

The main reason we use labels to justify ourselves, is because of 'avoidance'. It is far easier to stay as we are and avoid all the risks associated with growth. We basically fear failure and rejection.

All limiting self labels keep us locked in a past that is dead and gone. They are the result of resisting change, and believing that personal growth is not possible or desirable.

It is far easier to label ourselves than to take the risk of change. But the only constant thing in this universe is change, whether we like it or not. By reaching out and taking risks and trying new things, we not only learn, we also learn to enjoy. Change is the essence of life, and self labels suppress our natural urge to change and grow.

3. PREJUDICE SYNDROME

Prejudice is a behaviour that judges everyone that is different from oneself as strange, evil, bad, weird, stupid and so on. On the positive side, we may see someone we love dearly as larger than life, or as having an unreal purity, because we refuse to acknowledge anything negative about them. This is often seen with 'in-laws' siding with their own son or daughter against a marriage partner in a dispute, irrespective of circumstances.

Prejudice literally means that we pre-judge others based on how we view them from a limited point of view. Limited, because the action of passing a negative valued judgement on another, shows that we are viewing only a part of that person, (a gross lack of true understanding) and that if we were viewing the 'whole' person, criticism would not be necessary or possible. Unfortunately, however, if they are in any way different to how we look, think, speak or do things, then they are branded as different and to be avoided as undesirable.

Hence people of different races, religions, political groups, different age groups, homosexuals, weirdos, etc. are pigeon-holed as a different class 'type', and therefore suspect.

This keeps us within our own 'group'; people we feel comfortable with. But this restriction of certain people works against us if we harbour prejudice, because we are cutting off 90% or more of the population. Most other people are different in some way, which makes everyone refreshingly individual.

We may be limiting ourselves in this way because of the prejudices passed on from our parents, teachers, etc., or self conditioning which is preventing us from exploring new areas of growth and ideas. Prejudice is based less on hate of a person or group, and more on a fear of having to change *our* ideas. We don't approach an unusually dressed stranger to make conversation, because we may have already branded him as different, and our conditioning tells us that anyone different is difficult to cope with. The non-acceptance of another person reflects an area of non-acceptance in ourselves. We can't be bothered, and so dismiss a person with a whole range of experiences, beliefs, feelings, and ways of doing things, that as someone we can possibly learn from.

The human race is such a marvellous diversity of culture, beliefs and social approaches, that we have much to share and discover. Yet we separate ourselves with physical, national, geographical, religious and idealistic boundaries and view each other with suspicion and prejudice. The idea that 'we are better than they are', keeps us separate, not only from our fellow man, but also from ourselves as individuals. *Ponder this.*

"There is more that binds men together than separates them."

4.   ANGER AND RESENTMENT

The feeling of anger is experienced when our expectations and demands are not met. It represents a part of our life that we are not accepting and our reaction is one of anger and resentment. We probably don't like this reaction, and neither does anyone else around us at the time.

All of us have a set of rules, ideas and beliefs, by which we live. When other people intrude and do not fit exactly into our structure of how things should be, we react by getting upset and angry. It is an expectation and a demand that the world and the people in it should be the same, should be more like us in our way of doing things and fitting in with our structure of beliefs.

Anger is a choice, as well as a habit, and is a learned reaction to frustration. It manifests itself as hostility, rage; from verbally or physically striking out at someone, to a boiling silence. It is not just an irritation or an annoyance, but a feeling of seething, hostile, inner turmoil.

Our excuse for lashing out when we feel angry is that we think it's better to express it rather than bottle it up and get ulcers. But it would be more effective if we applied the five components of Rebirthing to our feelings of anger, rather than dumping all our hostility on everyone we meet. Remember, expression does not integrate the suppression.

With repeated practice of new thinking, thinking that assumes responsibility, acceptance and love for everything in our lives, we can eliminate expectations that demand others to be more like us.

5. GUILT AND WORRY

Most people suffer from these two futile emotions. Guilt for what has happened in the past, and worry for what might happen in the future. Guilt and worry are connected, and are really the opposite ends of the same problem of not being in the here and now; the present moment.

The present moment is wasted with guilt, dwelling in the past, while worry clings to the future. They are identical in as much as they upset our present moment with trying to correct a situation in a different time (past or future), which does not exist in the now. Robert Jones Burdette wrote in 'Golden Day':

"It isn't the experience of today that drives men mad. It is the remorse for something that happened yesterday, and the dread of what tomorrow may disclose".

Guilt comes from believing that we have done something wrong, and by choosing to feel bad about it, will somehow make it right. So, rather than choose to be happy, we sabotage our present moment happiness with feelings of guilt, in the hope that we will be forgiven.

Worry is a fear of the 'what if' syndrome. "What if this happens and what if that happens." It makes as much sense to upset our present moment happiness with 'what ifs', as it does with worrying about something that may happen in a thousand years. A good way to see the futility of worry is to ask ourselves, "Will this outcome make any difference in a hundred years time?" 99% of the time the answer will be *no*.

With understanding we begin to see the senselessness of making

111

our present moments uncomfortable by thinking about what happened last week, last year, or what may or may not happen tomorrow.

The habit of guilt and worry can be overcome by concentrating on the present moment, and a determination to free ourselves from useless thoughts of another time which have no relevance to being here NOW!

6. JEALOUSY

Jealousy is an emotion that has expectations on how other people should act towards us. We demand that someone love us in a certain way and feel resentful and hurt when they don't.

Jealousy stems from a lack of self confidence and a comparison of people with ourselves. When someone we love responds to another person in an affectionate or loving way, we experience jealousy. We feel they are comparing us with whoever they are now with, and feel slighted and ignored. But they are just being and loving ("the bastards!") But seriously though, it is ourselves who are experiencing the resentment, because we imagine that the person we love is preferring someone else over us. Because we lack self love, this imagined rejection results in the emotion of jealousy. But if we truly loved ourselves, we can see that it is alright for our partner to show affection for others, as our love for them and ourselves is unconditional.

Basically, jealousy is born when we claim ownership of other people. To regard our spouses, our children and those close to us as belonging to us, will certainly make us feel jealous when we are threatened by someone else attracting 'our' loved ones away from us. But jealousy is a childish attribute. We might as well try to own the sun or moon, than try and own another human being.

With understanding we can view what happens between someone we love, and someone else, as something between two people, rather than as something against us. Certainly, we can view it as a situation that is totally unrelated to our own self-worth.

A milder form of jealousy is envy. Envy manifests itself when other people have bigger, better or more of something than we have, and we feel resentful because of it. Envy is a similar emotion to jealousy, because they both stem from an ownership mentality, and we feel envious when everyone receives a present and we miss out. Being free of attachment to possessions and people, while being closely involved with them, is the secret to overcoming these debilitating emotions of jealousy and envy, which was anciently referred to as covetousness.

7. NEED FOR SECURITY

The need for 'security' in the context we are discussing here, means external assurance of always having certain possessions, money, a house, car, a spouse or someone to take care of us; someone who will make all those difficult decisions for us, solve our problems and make us happy. But security based on externals is another myth and a trap. Situations and people change, which can cause us to lose all our possessions and money, and people close to us can die or move away.

The need for 'security' is a learned conditioning hang-over from childhood. It is based on fear and a lack of self-trust, which is born from a lack of self-knowledge. Self-knowledge is the understanding of the great potential, latent within each of us, which enables us to totally trust ourselves, finding lasting happiness and feeling absolutely secure. This is the Internal Strength which is the True Inner Self. Because so few of us have yet developed our inner essence, which is the only true security that exists, we tend to place our trust in things and people external to us, which eventually always leads to disappointment and despair.

Most people are controlled by the externals in their lives. The word 'externals' as it is being referred to here, means anything outside ourselves which makes us feel a certain way, think along certain lines or do things that we would not choose to do ourselves had the outside agency not been present. Because we are controlled by these externals, and our conditioning reinforces our motivation to conform, we equate all our happiness and well-being to what is happening in our external world. Therefore, if we are unhappy, we try to make ourselves happy by changing things in our external world. This is like painting the outside of our house and hoping that the inside will look better.

Internal security and happiness are found where they really are— inside us. We will not make one ounce of difference to our internal happiness by changing our job, our spouse, friends, lover, place we live, environment, or whatever. If we are feeling bad, moving away from something won't make us feel any different. Momentarily it might, but the old longing and emptiness soon catches up with us, because we take ourselves with us wherever we go. The reason we feel bad is because we have separated ourselves from truth and truth is unconditional bliss.

By placing our trust in the externals around us, rather than ourselves, we begin to grow dependent upon these externals, and when

113

they are people, the slide into emotional dependency is almost automatic.

8.   HERO WORSHIP

Hero worship is a behaviour that again focuses on other people, by making someone else more important than ourselves. By admiring others greatly we can set them up in our mind to determine our own values. There is nothing wrong in admiring the virtues of others, but by trying to be like them denies the fact that we are also beautiful and important. We may have covered our beauty with some mental junk, but we learn nothing by imitating others. We only learn when we are our own heroes and are willing to take the responsibility for our own feelings, actions and thoughts.

Most of us need teachers only in so far as they guide us to be our own teacher. Sheldon B. Kopp wrote a book called "If you Meet the Buddha on the Road, Kill Him!". His message is that no meaning emanating from outside of ourselves is real, and that the trust and knowledge in each of us has already been obtained, thus we need only recognise it.

He writes:

"The most important things that each man must learn no one else can teach him. Once he accepts this disappointment, he will be able to stop depending on the therapist, the Guru, all who turn out to be just another struggling human being."

Teachers and Gurus who demand allegiance and love and promote hero worship of themselves by their devotees, are trapped in the ego trip game, but worse, they are teaching their followers to demean themselves and become dependent.

Our favourite Gurus, teachers, lovers, singers, actors etc., are only people who are good at what they do and are like us in as much as they fart, have body odour, defecate, make mistakes, are irritable, have certain weaknesses as well as strengths, but are no better (or worse) than ourselves.

Being our own hero is not an ego trip. The egotist is someone who hates himself, and is straining hard to get people to love him.

Once we develop self confidence and self love we realise that there is no greater (or lesser) hero than oneself.

9.   PROCRASTINATION

Putting things off rather than facing a situation is common with most of us. The problem areas in our lives, particularly those that involve people closest to us, are the one's we most avoid. We think that by bringing things out into the open feelings may get hurt, and so we keep them buried in the hope that they will go away or come right eventually. At best, things change, but they never get better on their own. Circumstances, events and people need our attention.

I worked with a woman in Rebirthing who had a 14 year old daughter who kept running away from home and finally got pregnant. She openly faced every aspect of why her daughter kept wanting to leave home, until the idea that her husband might not love his daughter was suggested. Over four weeks of counselling she skilfully avoided this issue everytime I mentioned it, and finally got angry with me after I brought it up for the third time. Only when she finally faced this possibility, which she had secretly feared all along, and found the courage to discuss it with her husband, did things improve. He agreed to get Rebirthed himself, and the whole problem was eventually resolved, due to her bringing her fears out into the open.

Problems and decisions that need our attention never just go away. We may bury, avoid or ignore them, but they keep coming up, reminding us that a part of our lives needs attention. The moment we avoid them, the more intense they become and the more anxious we start to feel. The point is, the reason a decision needs to be made or something comes to our attention to be done at a certain time, is because that very time is the best time to do it. Do it Now!

RIGHT VS WRONG CATEGORISING:

Avoid categorising the consequences of a decision into right or wrong.

I discovered I had a procrastination problem when a friend asked me if I had difficulty in making decisions. I answered, "Well, yes and no." My fear of decisions was always focused around doing the right thing and not making a mistake. My biggest mistake was the fear of making mistakes, yet it was the mistakes in my life that I learned from.

It finally dawned upon me that there is no right or wrong decision. No matter what I decided about anything, either way would promote a different outcome which was neither good nor bad, only different. The only way I could make a decision wrong, was not to make one at all (which is a form of a decision in itself) by avoiding any responsibility for my life. Once I gave up the erroneous ideas about good and bad, right and wrong, or even better and worse, decision making became easy. No matter what I decided, it would be the correct thing for me to do at that time. I would be doing the right thing at the right time in the right place.

When we overcome our self-sabotaging fear of the duality of right and wrong, we will find decision making a simple question of weighing up the pro's and con's, and preferences. If the results are different from those which we expected, then, rather than regretting a 'wrong decision', we can learn from the experience and resolve to make another decision in our next appropriate 'present moment'.

One last point about decision making. If it was possible to make a so-called wrong decision, the universe would change to fit in with our decision making, which shows that it can never be a wrong decision. Remember, we create our own Reality.

CHAPTER 19

THE 10TH SELF-SABOTAGE CONDITIONING: THE BLAMING AND 'NOT FAIR' SYNDROME.

We may be highly programmed to expect justice, equality and fair treatment in life and when it doesn't happen we feel frustrated, angry and cheated. Why do we feel this way when we experience unfairness in our lives? Perhaps it is because that fairness and justice does not really exist at all. That it is only a human concept that everything has to be fair so as to fit our individual structure of rules of right and wrong; that it is an expectation from externals in our life and people that they behave exactly like us, so as to fit our perception of how the world *should* be. But few things fit neatly into our structure because everything constantly changes and everyone is different. It seems that our demand for fair play has little relevance to the reality of life with untimely death, accident, war, crime, famines, floods, disasters etc., and suggests that fairness all the time is a myth. Half the world is starving while a small minority live in luxury. That doesn't seem fair. A disaster can strike a community without warning. Is that fair? One country invades another, one group of people oppress another group, crime is on the increase, all of which seems to demonstrate that demanding fairness is an external concept and a way of upsetting ourselves for no good reason.

The world and the people in it seem unfair to each other a lot of the time and that is the way the world is. We can either choose to react with anger and unhappiness or respond with happiness which has no relation to the lack of fair treatment we see, but depends upon our degree of inner self acceptance. The point is, that desiring rather than demanding justice is perfectly fine. It is only self-sabotaging when we feel bad as a result of ourselves or others not receiving it. Expecting and demanding is an addiction and must be fulfilled, whereas preferring justice is natural. If we remain centered, then our world isn't going to fall apart when we are treated unfairly.

Most of us, however demand fairness in all our relationships with others. 'You have no right to do that if I can't,; 'Would I do that to you?'; 'It's not fair.' We demand fair play, justice and equality and when we don't get it we feel justified in feeling angry, anxious and unhappy. Yet the desire for justice is not wrong, and we can work towards improving justice and equality (while at the same time remaining detached enough from being swept up emotionally) by choosing not to be upset by any injustice we see around us. It is only neurotic when we upset ourselves over what is happening externally to us. We punish ourselves by hitting ourselves over the head with negative emotions when our demand for justice from other people is not fulfilled.

Some people run relationships like a points system. If you have one, then I must have one. Everything has to be fair. You can see children fighting over one of them having one more sweet than the others. And you can see grown up children disputing pay rates, mineral and oil rights, international boundaries and so on. We may have all of something we need, but if someone else has more than us then we feel resentful. But no amount of complaining and feeling bad about it adds one drop to our personal growth as an individual.

Many protestors against the injustices of the world are genuine and compassionate folk, while others want to fight and force their brand of so called 'liberation' on to the rest of us. History has proved that such liberators usually replace one set of injustices with another. The desire to get even with those who have crossed us keeps us trapped in a low level of consciousness, for revenge cures nothing. The demand for fairness works only one way: 'what I want!' If we demand justice with conditions attached, like 'The rights of the people are paramount, (so long as they all think as we do)', we are implying the denial of justice to those who differ from us.

Justice is a concept of externals, and a way of avoiding taking charge of our own lives. Rather than think that anything is unfair by comparison with and thinking how unfair something or someone is, we can choose what *we* want and then set about achieving it, independent of what others think or do. It is not the unfairness that is important, but the way we respond.

THE BLAMING SYNDROME

Complaining about events, situations and people and attributing blame is one of the most self-sabotaging behaviours that inhibit our growth and happiness. By attributing blame, we are shifting our focus on to others and external events rather than looking inward to discover the cause of our frustration and unhappiness. This of course suits our ego very well, and we have a ready excuse as to why the world and the people in it are not giving us any happiness. We avoid all responsibility as to our part in it, and therefore we can easily blame all outside events and people for the way we feel. If things don't suit us then it is easy to blame someone else.

Almost everyone you meet has a bag full of blames as to why he or she can't find happiness or get enough of anything: 'my spouse doesn't understand me; my children don't respect me; my parents mistreated me; my teacher was unfair with my marks; the unions are too militant; management are out for all they can get', and the most popular of all when we run out of excuses — blame the government.

By blaming agencies outside ourselves we are denying the truth that thoughts are creative and that we create our own reality. As this is so then the people in our lives are acting towards us in a certain way because our thoughts and vibrations at a subtle level are influencing them to do so. If we are receiving a lot of 'shabby' treatment from others, instead of complaining and dishing out blame, examine what it is we are doing and thinking to contribute to the situation.

Years ago I had an inferiority complex about being short and thin, and therefore generally disliked myself. I couldn't understand why everyone I met, after a short time began treating me exactly the same way I was treating myself. I discovered, on close examination of my thought processes, that I was unconsciously sending out subtle messages to everyone around me that I was no good and should be treated accordingly. They were picking up these 'between the lines', subconscious signals, and were moved by my influence to carry out my instructions, 'I'm a slob, I don't like myself so you won't like me either.'

Charisma is nothing more than the aura of a person who loves himself, and projects a high personal presence. If we walk into a room full of strangers, they will treat us exactly the way we expect to be treated. It is a rapport we feel with certain people that we can't explain but only experience. We project telepathically our thoughts, feelings and sensations outward in widening circles and people pick up this unspoken communication, and determine almost unconsciously how they should treat us.

Battered wives almost always have a history of being beaten by all the men in their lives, from their fathers onwards. People with low self-images have a history of being 'put down' or ignored.

People who are often abused, manipulated, disrespected, forced into roles they don't like, are people who have a life long experience of such treatment from most of the people in their lives. It has nothing to do with the people in their lives, but in the way they subconsciously project themseves.

So blaming others for what treatment we are receiving from them is absurd, because we literally teach people how to treat us.

Try this experiment: Get a friend to stand with his or her back to you so as not to be able to read your body language. Then without moving a muscle, project emotionally and mentally an openness to the world, joyous feelings of an outgoing exuberance. Then project a dampened down, folded in feeling of being repressed. Ask them to tell you when and in which state you are in at any time.

This works powerfully after practising physically stretching, reaching and folding and curling up exercises as in yoga.

Blaming others inhibits our growth because we focus on the 'wrongs' of others instead of looking inward to discover the cause of our own frustrations and unhappiness. If we bump our knee against a table, it is in the knee that we feel the energy — not in the table. And it is just as stupid to blame the table for being in the way of our knee as it is for blaming other people for the 'pain' we suffer when the world appears to mistreat us. But most of us do it every day. Blame is a hidden way of avoiding responsibility and communicating anger.

The blame syndrome was caused by us when we decided to adopt the duality of opposites that we discussed previously. The duality of right versus wrong mentality. This is most common in people whose feelings are controlled externally by other people. We may have divided our world into two neat extremes of good and bad, black and white, right and wrong. Few things fit this unreal concept and most people float somewhere in the grey areas.

The right versus wrong mentality insists that we must always be in the right which means of course, that others must frequently be in the wrong. Therefore we demand that they admit they are in the wrong. After all, *'It's only fair.'* It's got to be fair in our controlled structure of rules of right and wrong. This creates competitiveness, especially between husbands and wives, and is often expressed 'You never admit when you are wrong', which often causes a communication breakdown. But people are not wrong, they are different and view things from different points of view.

We hang onto this behaviour because, like most of the Self-sabotage behaviour in our lives, we avoid having to take responsibility for how we feel. It's far easier to look outside ourselves for an explanation as to why we are feeling bad. But by blaming everyone else we cease to grow. By refusing to participate in any fault finding gossip that projects blame to any outside agency, we can get on with the task of finding solutions to unanswered questions rather than sitting around conducting inquisitions as to who was at fault.

CHAPTER 20

THE 11TH SELF-SABOTAGE CONDITIONING : THE TYRANNY OF MUSTS, SHOULDS AND OUGHTS SYNDROME

We may be guided and even controlled by a set of rules without seriously evaluating their effectiveness to our growth, fulfillment and happiness. We may not even subscribe to the 'musts', 'shoulds' and 'oughts' in our life, but do so mechanically because we are conditioned into believing that these structures hold our world together. But the truth is that there are no musts, shoulds, oughts, laws, rules or traditions that apply 100% of the time. There are times when flexibility is more sensible. Rules are made for the benefit of the majority of people to provide a basis of safety, health and happiness for most of the time and are an important part of our civilised society. But the unthinking adherence to inappropriate rules creates anxiety, frustration and unhappiness, particularly if they are the consequences of our obeying conditioned musts, shoulds and oughts. A rule is unhealthy only when it interferes with healthy and effective behaviour.

By obeying a 'must' that is sabotaging effective behaviour we have given up our freedom of choice, and are allowing ourselves to be controlled by some external power.

Do musts, shoulds and oughts control our life? *Should* we always be courteous and kind to the people around us? *Must* we always be supportive and loving to our wife, husband or children or friends? - *Ought* we always do our best in all things and work hard? And when at any time we fail in one of these rules, do we feel guilty and bad? Perhaps we feel bad because the must has come from the expectations of others or even ourselves. Then we are controlled by externals because we fear what others will think of us. Even high self expectations are mostly born from needing approval from others because we are not fully self accepting.

The point is that we don't have to do anything. We don't have to go to work, we don't have to provide or look after our family, nor even get out of bed in the morning.

But we do these things because they are profitable to us and the alternative is unsatisfying.

The idea that we have to do something makes us irresponsible in that act. The person who is motivated by musts, shoulds and oughts will rarely be able to put their best into it and their actions are for the wrong reasons — to satisfy someone or something supposedly greater than themselves. This is motivation by fear. The person who is motivated by wanting to do something will always be more highly motivated than the person who feels he has no choice and there lies the difference.

Motivation by fear and need, or the adherence to some rule, will confine us to receiving rewards based upon our efforts, and the measure of these efforts will always be greater from those who 'want to', rather than those who 'have to'.

Motivation by want will enable us to get from life exactly what we need, enabling us to act responsibly because we are able to take charge of our own lives.

A must, should or an ought is the result of conditioning by external control and has been fed to us to keep us in line and to behave. It is more of the *'Not to trust yourself behaviour'*, and we probably have made it a part of our lives.

'Must nots' are as numerous as 'musts' and include: we must not be offensive, rude, angry, stupid, selfish, emotional, unsporting, unfair, jealous, prejudicial, and so on. If we break any of these unwritten rules then we are expected to feel ashamed, guilty and bad until we have shown enough remorse to be forgiven.

In reality, it's OK not to be dignified, to lose our composure, not to understand, not to be always friendly and cheerful. We are allowed to have any emotion we like including negative ones. It's alright to feel, think and do whatever we choose so long as we take full responsibility for our feelings, etc., and respect the freedom of others. It's OK to do anything. We don't have to prove anything to anyone, including ourselves.

By not accepting ourselves as we are, warts and all, stress and strain result in having to be someone we are not and trying to live up to an expectation of a must, should or ought.

Having certain rules and disciplines to live by is OK if they are designed to lead to personal fulfilment, growth and happiness. However, if they don't do this, then we are in the self defeating area, and quite possibly we hang on to this behaviour because —

1. We are more likely to win approval by conforming and being regarded as a 'good' person.
2. We can remain self righteous about ourselves and judgemental about those who are different and don't obey the rules.
3. Our musts and shoulds help us manipulate others into our way of thinking by imposing our restrictions on them.
4. Our obedience to external rules justifies staying as we are and avoiding the risk of change by assigning the responsibility to a should rather than to ourselves.

By focusing on a must, should or ought, we avoid having to think and work on ourselves. Don't think, just follow the rules. It takes the risk out of living but it also takes the fulfilment out of life, because we are not living but 'being lived' by a series of rules, regulations, laws and traditions. Happiness comes from being our own person and not through external control of what some person or book said.

We probably use many self-sabotage words and sentences every-day without thinking too much about them, but they are clues to un-conscious habits of self rejection. Subconsciously we use them to avoid change and justify staying as we are.

THE SELF-SABOTAGE OF BUTS, IFS AND WHYS:

The word 'but' is used as an excuse or a condition that is placed upon some situation or person. Consider the following:

"I love her but she makes me mad."

By exchanging the 'but' for an 'and', we change the connotation of the meaning, for 'and' is more accepting.

"I love her 'and' she makes me mad."

- "I'd love to go 'but' I don't have anything to wear." (conditional)
- "I like you 'but' why don't you..." (Judgemental)
- "Yes 'but', what if it rains tomorrow." (Externally controlled)
- "I'd like to but I don't know how." (Avoiding change)
- "He's nice 'but'..." (Non accepting)
- "If only I had done..." (Regret)
- "If you were different, I'd be happy." (Expectation)
- "If only..." (Wishing reality were different)
- "Why does it always happen to me?" (Feeling sorry for oneself instead of taking charge of one's own life)
- "Why didn't I do that when I had the chance." (Regret)
- "Why do you always do that to me?" (Blaming other people rather

than taking responsibility for our own creative thoughts and projections.)

THE SELF-SABOTAGE OF OTHER WORDS:
- I'm too old to change... *(avoiding change)*
- I'm too ugly ... *(non accepting)*
- It's too hot, cold, painful, etc... *(comparing)*
- It's never been done before ... *(self-limitation)*
- It never works when I want it to... *(choosing to feel upset)*
- They said it was impossible ... *(putting other people's opinions ahead of your own)*
- They won't let me ... *(externally controlled)*
- I am sorry... *(Constant apologies stem from feelings of guilt and are pleas for forgiveness which is approval seeking.)*
- We/they/us/you feel this way... *(hiding behind others and not being truthful and stating "I feel")*

EXTERNALLY CONTROLLED	INTERNALLY CONTROLLED
I shouldn 't do...	I don't want to...
I should do this...	I want to...
I have to...	I feel like...
I must ...	I can...
I will try ...	I will do...
I can't ...	I won't...
I feel obligated to ...	I choose to...

More self-sabotage words we may wish to eliminate from our vocabulary: *Unfair; Bad; wrong; suffer; impossible; problems; sin; pain; evil; fault; can't; ugly.*

By choosing to be our own judge and rely on ourselves, the world will stand ready to serve us in our growth to higher consciousness. By sticking to the rules, staying as we are, we sabotage our growth-potential.

CHAPTER 21

THE 12TH SELF-SABOTAGE CONDITIONING:
THE ANATOMY OF FEAR

Most of us have experienced fear in one form or another. Fear is part of the fight-flight syndrome which is a hang-over from our ancestral caveman days when staying alive was a daily chore. The emotion of fear is an important part of our survival mechanism which we call upon when in real danger, and without it we could never have survived as a species.

For instance, if we are walking along a cliff-top track and suddenly the track begins to give way, our reaction is a healthy fear response. We don't have to stand around and decide whether we should leap to safety or not. Our response is automatic and appropriate.

However, in our modern age where most of us are not under a constant threat to life and limb, too many of us react with fear as if we were under threat, and we perpetuate the fear response beyond healthy levels. Very intense fear is destructive and can cause muscle paralysis and even heart attacks for those who have heart problems.

Fear beyond the initial inherited response is a similar emotion to worry, where we enlarge upon something that is already there until the fear emotion controls us. It is an over-reaction which takes us from the present moment and serves no useful purpose; it merely wastes time and makes us feel 'terrible'.

Fear is believing in an unsafe universe, and is really crossing our bridges before we reach them. That is, we imagine the worst that can happen in a future time and feel the emotion about it now. We are in fact artificially creating the flight-fight reaction and indulging in self punishment.

Animal reaction to human fear is one of excitement which evokes the fight-flight response in them, and can even cause them to attack the human experiencing the fear. This is because the animal is picking up destructive vibrations which it interprets as 'hate', 'violence', 'fear', 'kill', and which in turn triggers its own safety mechanism. Thus it either flees or attacks for its own self preservation.

Animals are very receptive to human vibration whether they be positive or negative. There are numerous cases of wild animals appearing quite tame with some humans as they had no fear and only love for animals.

It is very rare for the North American Indians to be ever bitten by snakes because they regard them as a natural part of the environment but the rest of the population suffer from snake attacks because they fear them.

The over indulgence of fear is a habitual reaction, formed over the years, to frustration, worries, problems, and a belief that others can hurt us in some way.

We may experience fear when:

- we are in a dangerous situation (fear as the initial reaction is healthy)
- a loved one may be killed or injured
- we think we may lose someone or something
- we think we may appear foolish
- we think we may not be accepted or liked
- we face the unknown

My own experience of intense fear happened when I was an infantry soldier fighting in Vietnam during the 1968 Communist TET offensive.

I'll never forget it. Our platoon came under heavy fire from a unit of NVA (North Vietnamese Army) troops, who were highly trained, very motivated and well armed. The intensity of the fire-power ex change was beyond the imagination. We had been caught partly in the open but each one of us managed to find cover and return fire. I had dived into a thicket and couldn't see much but as I carried a grenade launcher (M79) I lobbed the odd grenade in the general direction of the enemy. My adrenalin was pumping madly as I struggled to keep calm. I looked around and saw our platoon Commander, Lt. Wilson, waving frantically for me to run over to him as his position offered a better field of fire. I looked at the 30 metre clearing that separated us which was being torn up by enemy bullets, and the total paralyzing power of fear swept over me. I felt nauseated, my throat constricted and I couldn't move a muscle. I was completely petrified. A thousand thoughts scrambled my brain, including the vision of the numerous mutilated bodies I had seen in the preceeding months. I pictured myself looking that way and felt even more nauseated.

I looked at the boss again and his waving was even more frantic. I resigned myself to die, used every ounce of will-power I had, picked myself up and sprinted across the clearing. I couldn't believe that I made it across without getting hit, and in throwing myself on the ground I unknowingly knocked my grenade launcher sights out of plum. I fired off a round at a now retreating enemy, but with my sights out, the grenade hit a branch two metres in front of me, bounced and landed just ahead of our forward positions. But it didn't explode as these grenades don't arm themselves until they have travelled a certain distance. I was terror struck. I buried my face in the soft red dust, sobbing and struggled with my sanity.

I then seemed to pass through the terror and nothing mattered anymore. I became aware of the physical sensations of fear happening in the various parts of my body and began to detach myself and view me as if I was objectively looking at someone else. A great calmness came upon me. I slowly lifted my head, deliberately re-adjusted my sights and calmly began delivering grenades towards the general area of jungle the North Vietnamese had disappeared into. I never experienced such intense fear again.

This experience taught me that fear is an initial automatic response, which occured after I have fed into my computer (brain) thoughts that I was in danger, and this reaction is an ancient conditioning. But the paralyzing fear that followed was self inflicted. I imagined such terrible things and perpetuated the initial fear reaction which made myself fearful. Each time we came in contact with NVA units (and for the next five days we averaged three contacts daily), I monitored my fear response. I discovered that the time between the initial automatic fight-flight reaction of the first shot being fired and the instant of my feeling calm inside, shortened with each consecutive battle. By the time my tour was over (four months later) I had reduced the interval down to about two seconds and was approaching the point where I was overcoming the fear conditioned response altogether.

Had I reached this point, I doubt whether I would have survived Vietnam at all. For fear is an important survival tool in such extreme cases. However, extreme fear is not, because it can immobilise our whole muscular system, causing us literally to become frozen with fear.

But how many of us are faced with such life and death situations in our everday life? Yet, how many of us experience the gut tightening, nerve shattering, creeping paralysis of fear? Most of us, it seems, have areas in our lives where we experience fear as a result of thought rather than the response to physical danger.

Our caveman ancestors had to deal with ferocious animals to stay alive, whereas our fearful situations are abstract, that is, we have to deal with the ferocious animals of the mind, such as negative thoughts and emotions. We are fearful when we are unable to keep up payments on our car; are facing an uncertain future after a broken relationship; considering the prospect of being fired from our job; and so on. How can we overcome this debilitating response which probably kills more people through stress than all the other negative emotions put together? Simply by becoming aware of how we are feeling at the time we are feeling it.

A way to overcome fear is to discover its anatomy. The cause of fear in everyday life situations is created by unrealistically imagining an undesirable outcome to some event or circumstance. It is picturing in our mind some future event going wrong and thus dwelling on this non-existent event inducing the fight-flight syndrome and extreme fear.

Fear becomes a habit and our conditioned mind replays the memories of past disappointments, pains and failures and acts as a reminder that similar experiences are likely to happen again. Shakespeare expressed the results of fear when he said:

"Our doubts are traitors and make us loose the good we might win by fearing to attempt."

My own experiences in Vietnam showed me that I perpetuated my own fear by focusing my imagination on the penalty of failure which in that case was being killed or maimed. But in everyday life people are 'screwing' themselves up by dwelling on the possible outcome and penalty of failure or non-achievement. This is more easily explained in the following analogy.

Imagine if a friend told us that if we walked along a plank of wood 20cm wide by 6 metres long which lay on the ground to pick up a $20 bill at the other end none of us would have any problem doing this. But imagine if our friend placed one end of the plank on a ten storey building and the other end on an adjacent building and asked us to walk the plank to pick up an easy $20. How many of us would do it? Now suddenly a new element has entered the situation — a drop of ten storeys. Whilst the plank was on the ground we focussed upon the reward of $20. However, with the fear of falling ten storeys the reward for sucess is not sufficient incentive and the penalty of failure is too great. The fear of falling takes hold and makes this simple task seem impossible. It is the same with life situations. When we dwell on the penalty of non-achievement, we create it, and this is the key to overcoming fear.

Instead of dwelling on an unfavourable outcome, we focus on the desired results. That is why we use affirmations to facilitate this. You see, the opposite end of fear is what we want. We want happiness but we fear unhappiness. We want prosperity but we fear poverty. We want love but we fear loneliness. We dwell on the penalty of not achieving what we want. We can easily turn fear around by dwelling on exactly what we do want.

I remember my early rugby days when our team was competing in the final match of the competition against a side that was equal to us in competition points. With five minutes left on the clock, and the score at nine points each, we had to do something to pull this game out. I was half-back and about to put the ball in the scrum on our 22 metre mark with ourselves on defence. I put the ball in, ran to the back of the scrum and as the ball came out I heard our coach yell encouraging instructions "Don't pass to your first five eight." The message ran in my brain — 'don't pass to Ken', the opposite to that is — 'too late, I passed it'. The opposing half-back intercepted the ball and scored beneath our posts, costing us the game. To this day I have wondered why our coach instructed me in that instance, the way he did. Why would anyone instruct on how not to do something, or negatively rather than positively? Why would anybody motivate anyone or themselves with the reverse of an idea?

And so it is with fear. We dwell on the reverse of what we really want. Unfortunately most of us do this every day.

Self-realised people know that all of their actions will be governed by their dominant thoughts and that pain is the result of dwelling on the reverse of an idea of what they want.

By focusing on what we want rather than what we don't want leads to success in any endeavour, because we create our own reality and the dominant thought in our consciousness must reproduce itself through the use of psycho-cybernetic principles. That's why we can't lose weight if we keep thinking how fat we are, or get rich financially if we are continually worried about the bills, or find love in our life if we keep repeating to ourselves that no-one is ever going to love us.

We need to replace our fears with what we want and it's not very difficult. Our fear of poverty can be replaced with wanting affluence.

Our fear of failing in some event can be replaced with wanting to succeed. We need to focus on the reward of success that we want rather than on the possible penalty of failure. We need to focus on the solutions rather than the problems, the answers rather than the questions, because when we fear an outcome we are setting it up to be our goal. We need to make our wants our predominant thought and we will overcome the paralysing effects of fear forever.

If you, the reader, have reached this part of the book, still experience fear in your life and are not using affirmations, then I suggest you go back and read Chapter 12 again.

Once we banish fear from our lives, we reach a state of consciousness which can best be described as 'BEING'.

'BEING' is a state of consciousness that is conscious of Itself. 'BEING' is simply being in the present moment, totally unconcerned with fear or wants. 'BEING' understands that all that is necessary has already been achieved, all that is needed is already obtained, all that will be, already is. 'BEING' is the state of consciousness that has transcended all experience and has Realised Itself and It's completeness.

Remember, the initial response of fear which occurs when we are in danger is normal and healthy and it only becomes counter-productive when we continue to choose to feel that way.

PART THREE

THE ART OF LEARNING, LOVING AND LIVING.

CHAPTER 22

SELF LOVE

Modern psychology has revealed that each of us has an idea of the person we think we are, a mental blue-print as it were, or a picture of the person we imagine ourselves to be. Some call it the self-image or ego and it may be vague and not clearly defined, but it exists, right down to the last detail. This self-image is the conception that we have of ourselves, our personal belief of the sort of person we each think we are.

This self-image or ego has been created by our own beliefs about ourselves which have been formed mostly unconsciously from our past experiences; our successes and failures, the feelings and thoughts we create in any given situation, our past behaviour and how other people have responded to us. It is from these that we mentally create a picture of ourselves and once a belief about this imagined self gets fixed into this picture, we become conditioned into believing it to be true. We don't even question how valid it is and our behaviour always responds to this self-image as if it were true and so the self-image, which is nothing more that a collection of thoughts and feelings about ourselves, controls every aspect of our lives. Every action, feeling, behaviour, ability and our personality is based on this conditioned self-image that we have of ourselves. In other words we will always behave in conformity with the person we imagine ourselves to be. In fact, in spite of all conscious effort to behave differently we simply cannot do so. If you doubt this ask yourself if you could leap on top of a table in a busy restaurant and do a little dance. Most people couldn't imagine themselves doing such a thing outside the mind.

If through our personal law (which is responsible for all our conditioning) we conceive ourselves to be a person who never succeeds at things or who finds achievement generally difficult, we will always find some way to fail. No matter how much will-power, conscious effort and good intentions, we will unconsciously create circumstances that will be consistent with our belief.

This self image is a foundation on which our entire personality, our entire behaviour is built. Not only this, but our every circumstance will also be totally affected in the same way. Remember — we create our own Reality from our thoughts and our thoughts come from a conditioned mind, which is the basis of our self image. It is because of this that our Reality and experiences seem to verify our belief, which further strengthens the belief of the type of person that we think we are. Thus a circle of events continues to run our lives in a similar pattern.

Everything in our life is connected to our self image in one form or another. This often restricts us operating our lives effectively.

In our present level of awareness, the self image is the key to our personality, our behaviour and our circumstances. By changing the self-image, we change the personality behaviour and our circumstances. It is the self image that sets the limits of our accomplishments. It controls us in what we can or cannot do. By developing or expanding the self image, we expand the dimension of what we believe we can accomplish. You see, the self image is the controlling device in any human endeavour for people operating on the 'normal' level of consciousness. 'Self-Realisation' is operating on a higher level of consciousness which we will discuss shortly.

Humankind's greatest single problem is clinging to a false sense of self, of well rehearsed social roles that keep him confused and prevent him from knowing who he really is. People are chained by their misunderstanding of happiness. A person is chained by a marriage, a compulsive ambition, a reputation, a certain role and so on. They limit themselves to what they believe they are, yet they are none of these things.

They are pure centres of perfect bliss who don't give two cents for being famous, or rich or loved; the centre of a person's being is all these things and more.

In creating a self-image we look out to our exterior world in search for what we already are inside.

'Self-Realisation' is achieved by passing through three stages:
1. SUBCONSCIOUS SUFFERING — where our suppressions manifest themselves as physical illness, depression, fear, phobias, etc.
2. CONSCIOUS SUFFERING — where we activate our suppres-

sions, consciously feel them and change our perception towards them.
3.   INTEGRATION — in which full awareness of our self conflict has dissolved our ego and we are in touch with our higher SELF.

Rebirthing is about eliminating the conditioning of our past by integrating the 'made wrong' decision about certain experiences which come about through a false self-image.

'Self-realisation' is going beyond our self-esteem and our self-contempt. This means that we cease from dividing the mind with opposing ideas about ourselves. The mind occupied with self-esteem will be vain, while a mind engrossed with self-contempt is denying the truth within. Both positions are false because they are both the same in as much as that both minds seek the truth outside themselves. 'Self-realisation' is above these opposites and comes about when our invented selves are integrated in the light of understanding, acceptance and love.

The state of 'Self-Realisation' never needs to be defended or protected because there is nothing to protect. Only the illusory ego needs protection when it feels threatened and only the ego can feel threatened i.e. those labels with which we identify ourselves. It is in trying to protect what we call 'ourselves' that we create tension in the mind when someone insults us or is rude, or criticises us. Integrating the ego frees us from ever feeling offended. After all what gets offended? Imaginary ideas of virtue or an attitude. By being offended we show that a particular attitude is only an idea. It is just as foolish to take offence as it is to give offence. Both are opposite poles of the same problem — a self-image. By daring not to defend our ego we in fact begin to integrate it and slowly begin to experience our inner truth.

It is interesting to observe the people around us. We can see how confident and happy they sometimes appear, while in almost every case they are simply imitating the contrived cheerfulness of others, being unconsciously absorbed in the artificial atmosphere. That is why 'partying' is so popular. Put these people among depressed people and their subconscious minds put out the signal 'time to be depressed', which they slavishly obey. Such people are controlled by the surroundings and never by themselves.

The self-image distorts and screens out all incoming impressions according to our conditioned personal desires and motives, thus creating a block between us and reality. With the integration of the self-image, we no longer divide good from bad, likes from dislikes etc., but see everything as a perfect free-flowing exchange between us and external events.

We must begin to see that we are not our acquired opinions, ideas, beliefs, habits or material possessions. We are 'the way, (intellect), the truth (emotions) and the life' (physical body) that Jesus spoke of.

There is nothing more that has to be added to us to make us complete. We are already complete. We merely have to chip away at our conditioning to free our inner true SELF, the same way that the sculptor chips away at a slab of marble. The sculptor does not put anything material into the marble to make a fine statue but simply subtracts the unwanted marble.

Most of us identify ourselves with our conditioning (the unwanted marble surrounding our perfect statue), the husk we have encased ourselves in for protection. It is a form of protection against an imagined hostile world. Yet we fear losing this conditioning (ego) through Rebirthing, for having identified with the ego, we fear its ending will be our ending. It is the ending of this conditioning which is our very deliverance from unhappiness but this will not be seen until we dare to see it. The awareness of our conditioning can lift us above a conditioned self-image.

A person often rejects knowledge of what he needs to know. He feels uncomfortable with the idea of inner change because it is a threat to his ego — his already established self-image; of being a person who believes he already knows and understands. Yet it is these self-images which appear to give a person individuality, actually keep him trapped and psychically asleep.

Socrates once said that 'Slanderers do not hurt me because they do not hit me'. Socrates was 'Self-realised' and had got rid of his collection of anxious ideas we call 'I'. If we have no subconscious self-image of being a failure or a success, of being mediocre or important, we cannot be hurt by how people respond to us. If we do not imagine ourselves as being loved or unloved by others, how can we be distressed when others reject us.

All this considered however, too many people are walking around with a negative self-image of self-rejection, self-dislike and downright self-hate. We can talk all day about reaching 'Self-Realisation' but if we dislike ourselves in any form, we can't even get to first base. How can we possibly take the first step forward if we sabotage ourselves by a fear of stumbling, expecting to hear our ego say, 'I told you so, you'll never make it', when we do stumble. We need to start loving ourselves first before we can ever hope to clean out the ego. If we hate ourselves, then our subconscious mind will keep us in that old cycle of self rejecting behaviour, which reinforces our negative self concept.

If we are unconsciously hitting ourselves over the head with self-rejecting behaviour and thoughts, then we need a massive dose of self-love, which reaffirms the truth that we are beautiful, lovable and important.

However, society has confused self-love with egotism, and this confusion has resulted mainly because so few people can really love themselves. This is projected through our behaviour with:-

- putting ourselves down with negative comments about ourselves like 'sorry you have to put up with me'.
- inability to accept a simple compliment directed at us with a simple 'thank-you' but instead we brush it off with embarrassment.
- putting others before ourselves with the hope that they will love us more, or thinking they are more important than ourselves.
- making other people's opinions more important than our own.
- always needing approval for everything we say or do.
- hero-worshipping some teacher, guru, or person we assume is higher than ourselves.
- disliking or hating certain persons (they are our mirror images) or group.
- disliking our physical body or part of it.
- rejecting the love from another person (how can they possibly love me?).
- inability to express our love or feelings to another person (spouse, parent, friend) for fear that they may not respond likewise or reject us.
- feeling guilty, ignorant or anxious when someone criticises us.
- feeling guilty or regretting some past experiences.
- fearing or worrying about some future event.
- reacting to criticism with counter-criticism.
- using words like should, must, ought, can't, but and too much.
- criticising others or always blaming someone for something.
- skimping on luxuries with an excuse of not being able to afford it when we really can.
- making our mates sexual satisfaction more important than our own.
- having to prove ourselves to others or even to ourselves.
- seeing a distinction between success and failure, fame or shame, happiness and depression.
- continually comparing ourselves with others and feeling jealous

and resentful.

- playing different roles depending upon which audience we are 'playacting' in front of; a role for our spouse, children, friend, our priest or vicar etc.
- having little interest or respect for others or their integrity.
- having a lot of physical sickness and ailments and general bad health.
- consuming junk food, alcohol, nicotine, drugs, not exercising or generally not caring for the physical body.
- being egotistical or conceited.

All these are tiny indications of self-hate.

This list could probably go on forever, and every time we engage in a kind of self put down behaviour, not matter how petty it appears to us, we reinforce our conditioning and create further a poor self-image. Those little negative comments we place on ourselves that surface during innocent conversations, those actions that deny us being beautiful, worthy and important are all indications of suppressed energy in the form of self-rejection.

So how do we feel about ourselves? For most people it will probably be pretty low in self-esteem. The self-image is not a single concept but is made up of many ideas, images and feelings. These ideas we have of ourselves cover our three functions — the physical, intellectual, emotional, and these take in our abilities in athletics, human relationships, learning, art and so on. Our self-concepts are as numerous as our activities and thoughts, and right at the centre is always ourself, the idea of the person we either love or hate. When considering whether we like ourselves or not we may tend to throw all our negative self concepts into a combined NO!

For this debilitating and self-limiting condition of self-hate, we need a massive dose of self-love.

Unfortunately society seems to regard self-love as wrong, egotistical or selfish. But this regard for our own self worth is not egotism unless it is confined exclusively for ourselves. Egotistical people are self-rejecting and basically selfish. They are only interested in themselves to the degree that they want everything only for themselves without regard for others. They feel no pleasure in giving, only in receiving and view the world only from what they can get out of it. They lack interest and sensitivity in the needs of others, have little respect for others dignity or integrity. They see nothing but themselves, being totally self-centred and their world is barren of any form of love.

Egotism and genuine self love are complete opposites. The egotist in fact hates himself and this lack of self appreciation leaves him empty and frustrated. In his unhappiness, he anxiously grabs from life the satisfactions which he blocks himself from attaining naturally. He appears to care too much for himself, but in fact he is making an unsuccessful attempt to cover up and compensate for his failure to care for his true inner self. And how can he act differently when he has been conditioned (or conditioned himself through suppressions) to react to a supposedly hostile world?

Conceit is another ego telling the world how wonderful we are in a vain attempt to win the attention and love of others by boastful or 'chest thumping' behaviour, while hating ourselves.

Egotism and conceit are just another subtle form of self hate. Genuine self love has nothing to do with building an ego. Conceit and egotism is trying to prove we are worthy while at the same time hating ourselves. Self love helps eliminate the ego because we no longer feel the need to prove we are superior or worthy.

There are those of us who appreciate the vastness of the universe, the beauty of a small child, a flower, or a sunset, and at the same time despise ourselves. Did we not come from the same source? Are we not, as a human being, at least the equal of all other wonderful creations?

The appreciation of our own worth is not egotism, unless we assume we are above or better than anyone else.

But our general self-rejecting behaviour is the result of our personal law and stems mainly from childhood, with such messages as 'think of others before ourselves' and that the idea of self love is selfish, arrogant, conceited and so on. As young children we loved ourselves naturally and regarded ourselves as very important and beautiful. But as we grew up, the messages from adults, teachers, relatives etc. have affected our natural self love and so self doubt became well established. Messages like 'you are so dumb', 'you bad girl/boy', 'Mother doesn't like you when you behave like that', rather than, 'Mother doesn't like the way you are behaving'. All too often an adult will verbally attack the child rather than the situation. We as children, after a while, began believing these statements to be true and began to live them as the habit was formed. So often we learn the conditionings of others at the expense of our own values. It is not suprising that we reach adulthood with many difficulties surrounding our own self-worth.

But how does our poor self-concept get in the way of living effective lives? In the vital area of loving others, OUR ABILITY TO LOVE SOMEONE IS BASED ON OUR ABILITY TO LOVE OURSELVES.

The more love we have for ourselves, the more love we have for others. In other words, love is an ability. Love cannot be exclusive to only one person or group or even to oneself. Either it is present or it is not. We cannot love one person while hating another. Love cannot be divided like that. Love has little to do with other people for it stems from our Inner Being. When love flows it touches everyone.

Everyone has a different concept of 'Love' and this is based on each person's level of consciousness, but we define 'love' as:

A willingness to accept others as they are without them having to satisfy us in some way;

A love that is totally ego free and unconditional.

A love that never demands another to be different or to be like us.

A love that never expects something in return for the giving of our affection, time, posessions etc.

A love that never craves something from another like sex,   money, comfort, support, security and so on.

A love that is totally giving and accepting.

How many of us can love like that? Very few, because there is always the insistance that others or another meet our expectations.

Yet by loving ourselves first, by feeling we are worthy, important and beautiful, we become secure enough in ourselves and begin to be able to give out. Only by accepting ourselves first are we able to accept others. The 'do-gooder', always putting others before himself is not loving, but is demonstrating self rejection and is secretly hoping that someone will love him in return. This self hater cannot love others because he usually expects total obedience from those he has 'sacrificed' so much for. When we are genuinely in love with ourselves, we are able to love and serve others, because the love for others is simply the surplus of the unlimited love we have for ourselves. We love others not for what we will get in return but for the pleasure we get from being a helper and a lover.

A person cannot love another beyond the love he has for himself. Orthodox religion has taught 'Love your neighbour as yourself'. Modern psychology suggests that to love yoursef enables you to be better able to love your neighbour.

George Bernard Shaw once said, 'A man's interest in the world is only the overflow of his interest in himself.'

William Shakespeare wrote this: 'To thine own self be true. And it must follow as the night and day, thou canst not then be false to any man'.

Goethe put it this way: 'The greatest evil that can befall man is that he should come to think ill of himself.'

My favourite fairy tale, Rapunzel, is the story of a young girl, imprisoned in a tower by an evil witch. The beautiful young girl, is continually told by the witch that she is ugly, which keeps Rapunzel in the tower a prisoner for fear of exposing herself. The day of her liberation occurs when from her window she sees standing down below, her prince charming. She throws down the end of her long golden hair and he climbs up to rescue her. The tower has nothing to do with Rapunzel's imprisonment, but the fear of her own imagined ugliness which has been described so often and conditioned her so effectively. Yet, when Rapunzel sees, mirrored in the eyes of her lover, that she is beautiful, she is finally free from the destructiveness of her own imagined ugliness. And we all have a witch inside telling us continually how ugly we are and we call it the self-image.

Who in this world is regarded as unworthy? The only people who fail, who are defeated, who are unworthy, are those who believe it of themselves. The only people who are despised by others, are those that despise themselves. Unworthiness is a self-inflicted illusion, of making something that is perfect, wrong, by denying its truth.

Regarding ourselves as unworthy and unloved makes giving love impossible. How can we give something away that we don't have to begin with? How can we love another while being devoid of love for ourselves? The whole question of giving and receiving love begins at home with persons who totally love themselves.

Love can not be separated or divided into love for this person and not for that person. Whenever we hate someone, we in fact hate all persons including ourselves because that person is merely acting as a mirror to what is inside us. No matter what happens out there in our exterior world, our reaction is simply the mirror of our conditioning. The person who says he hates war, crime and violence is reflecting his hatred and non-acceptance for something inside himself. This hatred is what perpetuates war, crime and violence. The person who accepts and loves every part of his experience, mirrors his inner love for himself. This is not to say that we should encourage war, crime and violence. But we should accept it as a part of the surface reality and love those who participate in them. Total compassion will be the only thing that will deliver the world from its negativities.

To love ourselves means that we are concerned with our growth, our happiness and will behave in ways which enhance these values.

We will care for our bodies, our minds and our feelings. By loving ourselves we actually practice the art of loving and thus are more effective in loving others.

By loving ourselves we become more attentive to our own needs and this increases our sensitivity to the needs of others.

We need to challenge all our negative feelings which prevent us from loving ourselves. Even when we have behaved in ways which have disgusted us, self hate will only perpetuate the feeling. Never is self loathing healthier than self love. Instead of rejecting ourselves, we can use all our negative behaviours as learning experiences which may need to be repeated until we have accepted and learned from them. Above all, never connect whatever we do or fail to do with our self worth. This is the key to self love. Let me say this again:

1. Never connect our self-worth with any negative thoughts and feelings we have about ourselves.
2. Never connect our self-worth with our behaviour.
3. Never connect our self-worth with the behaviour of others towards us.

Our self-worth is totally unrelated to our thoughts and negative feelings, our behaviour and other people's behaviour towards us.

This is because we are complete in ourselves and we don't need others to verify our worth by loving us. Our worth is determined by oneself, by us loving ourselves so much, that rejection or approval from others can never affect us. When others react to us negatively, it can often be an indication that we are hating ourselves at that time, particularly if we begin to feel bad as a result, but this has nothing to do with our worthiness.

Our worthiness has nothing to do with our behaviour, performance or feelings because feelings and behaviour come from a conditioned ego and not from our True Inner Self. We may do something that hurt someone else deeply; we may fail at some particular project; we may be subjected to verbal abuse by someone we care for; we may have performed in such a way which society condemns as bad; we may not like our behaviour in a particular instance. This does not mean that we are without worth. We must understand that our worth is quite separate from our achievements or failures. Without this understanding, we will probably confuse our real self with our external activities. Our self worth is no more connected to some outside activity as it is to how people think of us. Once this confusion becomes clear that we are valuable in spite of other people's disapproval and even our own, we can begin loving ourselves and even those people who once despised us.

The inability to love ourselves affects our self confidence and the ability to believe in ourselves. Belief in ourselves is synonomous with self confidence. 'Con-fidence' comes from a Greek word meaning 'with trust'. To develop self confidence, we need to learn how to trust ourselves and this comes about with self knowledge. We will begin to know ourselves only after we have an awareness of every part of us and have begun to accept and love every aspect of ourselves. This expansion of love for ourselves must extend to every other living form in the universe and is the means to our liberation. Nothing else will do it. Good deeds are secondary in comparison.

We can expand our love simply by loving whatever we are doing and love ourselves for performing that action; love whatever we are feeling and ourselves for having that emotion. Whatever our situation or circumstances are, love every aspect of it. By loving every experience as much as we can from wherever we are, will dissolve every negative feeling and will bring a new acceptance into our lives.

Love everything exactly the way it is. We cannot improve on perfection. We only make things 'wrong' when we try, and the result makes us feel negative. So let's love our negative feelings, our anger, our fear etc., and those times when we just cannot love something, then love ourselves for hating it.

The question of good or bad actions, thoughts or feelings doesn't arise because any activity, thought or feeling performed in full awareness and total love is perfect and transcends the duality of good and bad. The dimension of love is all that needs to be changed, and if we are unable to express our love or even feel it, then totally accept ourselves for not being able to. Acceptance of ourselves is the first step towards self love. As we grow more loving towards ourselves and others, we will begin to see every person, every object and situation as pure and perfect. Since beauty is indeed in the eye of the beholder, every moment will be a rich experience of pleasure and splendour.

The habits of self-rejection from our early years are not easily overcome, and our negative self-image may still be based upon how others respond to us and their opinions of us. As our original self image developed through the opinions and responses from the adults in our lives, we don't have to hang on to it any longer. We need only love and accept what we are, where we are, how we are and who we are with. Nothing else matters.

GEMS ALONG THE WAY:

- Every person has an ego or self-image which is the type of person he or she imagines themselves to be.
- The self-image is the result of our conditioning and makes us perform in a lot of unnecessary social roles in an attempt to be more acceptable.
- Most people hate themselves and the best known cure is a massive dose of self love.
- Our ability to love others is based upon our ability to love ourselves.
- Never connect our self-worth with any negative thoughts or feelings we have about ourselves.
- Never connect our self-worth with our behaviour.
- Never connect our self-worth with the behaviour of others towards us.
- We expand our love by loving whatever we are doing and love ourselves for performing that action; love whatever we are thinking and ourselves for having that thought; love whatever we are feeling and ourselves for having that emotion.

CHAPTER 23

SELF-ACCEPTANCE

Self love is only possible when we have begun to accept ourselves as an entirety.

By the time a child becomes a teenager, he is filled with fears, myths, and doubts about his own self-worth which schooling, and significant adults in his life, have impressed upon him. Some of the knowledge which certainly needs to be unlearned is: 'I am not important; my actions and feelings cannot be trusted and should be controlled; I am controlled by other people; permission must be given before I do things; my natural self needs to be covered with a certain mode of dress, cosmetics etc. to be acceptable; I must become what others say I should; I need approval from everyone; others are more important than I am; and so on and so on.'

What we want is an entirely new kind of acceptance. It is an acceptance which we do not even have to think about. To think about acceptance shows a lack of acceptance, for we are separating the person wanting love and acceptance and that of true self acceptance itself. We never think about water except when we are thirsty, and do not have any to satisfy us. True self acceptance is ours when the mind stops separating itself from itself. This creates a unified mind and integrates the false sense of self, which we wrongly think we are or must become. The Real Inner Self is composed of nothing but love and acceptance and needs nothing outside of Itself.

ACCEPTANCE OF OUR UNACCEPTANCE:

Often people who dislike themselves and want to change, go about it in a way which keeps them stuck in the self rejecting ways. In other words, they make a perfect situation 'wrong' by not accepting and loving themselves as they are, warts, wrinkles, thoughts, feelings and all. So they try to change themselves into a so-called 'better' person by taking on a new role of being a spiritual person, a kind, loving person, a giving person, or a healthy person, and so on. This type of self-change is motivated by a fear of not being loved and an inability to accept ourselves the way we were before, and so we try to be someone different, which is not being true to ourselves.

True self-change and true spirituality only happens when we totally love and accept our total self; which includes our body, our mind, our feelings and yes, even our ego. It is learning to become more like ourselves and accepting who we really *are*. We need only relax, enjoy life, live, love, be child-like at times by not taking ourselves too seriously, and above all, accepting our unacceptance. True Self-Acceptance begins when we start to accept that we hate a part of ourselves. At this stage, there will be things in our lives that we probably just cannot come to terms with, because we simply find those things distasteful and unpleasant. Good, then all we have to do is acknowledge that unacceptance. Nothing else. To pretend to like something while really hating it is merely playing another role and is a subtle form of suppression, of not being true to ourselves. If we dislike a part of ourselves say for instance our anger, or a part of our physical body, we can say to ourselves, 'One day I am going to love that but right now, I love myself for hating it.'

The key to this whole question of self-love and acceptance is relaxing, being our self and accepting our unacceptance.

The point is, self-acceptance is possible without having to reach some state of imagined perfection. Self-Realisation does not necessarily mean perfection, but instead, it offers us the ability to live with the acceptance of our imperfection. (Imperfection being the false and negative beliefs we have about ourselves and the world.) A perfectionist is someone who hates a part of himself but demands perfection from himself and those around him to cover up and compensate for his unacceptance.

Self-acceptance means coming to terms with ourselves now, just as we are, with all our faults, weaknesses, mistakes, shortcomings as well as our strengths. Self-acceptance is easier when we realise that all our negativities only belong to us; they are not us.

Self-acceptance becomes easy when we stop identifying ourselves with our mistakes. We may have made a mistake, but we are certainly not a mistake. True religion teaches that the first step towards salvation is the self-confession that we have 'sinned', as opposed to being a 'sinner'. We need to recognize our mistakes before we can correct them. The first step towards gaining knowledge is to recognize those areas where we are ignorant. The first step towards becoming strong is to recognize we have areas that are weak. In Rebirthing we use negative feedback in the way of activated suppressed energy to become 'Self-Realized'.

Rebirthing, along with many self-improvement techniques, talks about change which might suggest changing into a 'better' person, or into someone else. If this were true then the whole point would be lost. Healthy change is all about changing from the person we thought we were (conditioning) into the person we really are (freedom). To try and change into someone else who we perhaps admire, is impossible and only ends up in us role-playing and denying our true self. A healthy desire for change is when we want to grow and discover new experiences, rather than not accepting something about ourselves, or what or where we presently are.

If change is motivated by not accepting what we are, any change will be superficial and temporary, because we are suppressing a part of ourselves that we do not love. Thousands of people rush into the numerous self-improvement schemes around these days because they hate a part of themselves and wonder after a while, why the initial boosting effects do not last. Healthy change is motivated by a desire to discover more about ourselves, rather than the wish to change into another person.

I used to work for Self-improvement, now my aim is for 'Self-development'. Self-improvement suggests improving what we already are. As we are perfect, how can we improve upon perfection. Self-development is developing what we have hidden (our True Self) and needs only uncovering and bringing to the surface. We need to improve nothing, but instead develop who we really are: *Truth, Love and Joy.*

SELF-ACCEPTANCE V. INDIFFERENCE

While self-acceptance is loving ourselves at all times, indifference is *not caring what happens* and we become resigned to whatever befalls us. Indifference is *imposing* a total acceptance and is in fact a form of self-hate, and a withdrawal of our awareness away from life in general.

Self-acceptance recognizes that we have areas that need cleaning up and that we can love everything in our here and now situation, including our non-acceptance. Self-acceptance is being involved with life yet it is being non-attached to future 'outcomes', because being non-attached keeps us in the present moment. Indifference means we don't care what happens, because we don't feel worthy enough to experience happiness in the present or the future. This type of acceptance is based on self-rejection, and even extends to seeking punishment and situations where we may be hurt, like a poorly matched relationship. While indifference does not 'care less', and imposes a form of self-rejecting acceptance in the form of play-acting; self love *always* cares and enables one to be onself.

STEPS TO TOTAL SELF-ACCEPTANCE — THE KEY TO TOTAL LOVE

So far we have discussed the preliminary steps to self-acceptance, but let us get right down to the basic steps that, if followed, will give us total self-acceptance.

STEP 1:

Get rebirthed. The rest will follow naturally and easily if we begin to integrate our suppressions.

STEP 2:

Learn and practice every day some form of meditation or centering type technique. This will expand our consciousness, in order that we can discover new experiences within ourselves, and develop 'self-knowledge'. Without these first two steps, the next eight steps will be like paddling a canoe up a fast flowing river.

STEP 3: ACCEPTANCE OF OUR PHYSICAL BODY

We need to ask ourselves whether or not we accept and love every part of our physical body. If we don't, then we are rejecting that part of us which makes us human. If we reject ourselves physically or any other part of us, then we will also reject other human bodies which means other human beings.

We have all been conditioned by society's definition of what constitutes beauty. If you are a woman today, then a slim, well proportioned body and certain facial features are regarded as beautiful. Three hundred years ago today's beauty queens would have been regarded as too skinny, because a plumpish body was in vogue. Beauty contests and such like undermine our perception of what beauty really is. Whether or not we regard one body as beautiful and another as ugly is only our personal perception, which is based on our conditioning. Ugliness does not exist except in the confused minds of brain-washed people, which we all are to a greater or lesser degree.

Those things we dislike about ourselves, such as being over-weight, too short, or too tall, too thin, having hair in certain places, or a lack of it, a mouth which is too large, small or too large breasts, and so on, is simply a matter of our perception. We may not be able to change those things, but we can change the way we view them. Everything IS PERFECT AND NOTHING IS TOO ANYTHING.

Being short is no worse (or better) than being tall. Just different. All we have been doing when disliking our bodies, is confusing our perception of what society regards as beautiful and ugly, against that which is true. Remember, beauty is in the eye of the beholder and by seeing our physical body as beautiful, we are deciding to be independent of the comparisons and confused opinions of others. By deciding what is pleasing to ourselves, irrespective of what others may think, we can love our physical body and begin to discover the multitude of beautiful feelings and physical sensations within each of us.

Being human means that each of us is unique and we therefore have our own particular shape, size, colour, smell, growth of hair and so on. To compare one physical body with another makes as much sense as comparing a green apple with a red one. But society and industry encourages us to be ashamed and mask our natural human qualitites with 'camouflage' behaviour. TV and newspaper advertisements send out a continuous stream of messages saying that we should hide the real self with their 'new product', to dislike the way our mouth, skin, feet, underarms smell and that our face and hair need improving in order to feel good and natural again. We are led to believe that we shouldn't accept the way we are and that by using cosmetic odours, make-up, removing certain hair, etc., we will like ourselves better. This implies that the natural way we are is un-pleasant and that only by making ourselves artificial, can we become more acceptable.

It is not suprising that advertisers encourage this type of thinking in view of profits to be made, but it encourages us to be contemptuous of being a natural human being. It is no wonder most people have a lot of self-rejection towards their physical bodies and are confused about what beauty is supposed to be.

Self love is about accepting our entire physical self and experiencing the beauty of being natural without the need to try and impress other people. If we are not beautiful to others, it is not because we are not beautiful, it is because they have a hang-up within themselves which is confusing their perception of beauty. However, we can always feel beautiful by simply loving ourselves.

Maxwell Maltz, a plastic surgeon in the United States and author of "Psycho-Cybernetics", once said that you can never change the inner self by changing the outer self. He once had a woman client with a badly crooked nose. After the plastic surgery he got the woman to look into the mirror which revealed a face that would grace any movie star convention. She looked at it and said, 'it might be beautiful, but I still feel ugly inside.'

That is the conditioning we have to overcome and it is easy when we are using Affirmations and getting Rebirthed. We can love our physical body so much, and derive so much pleasure from it, once we have eliminated the ideas that we need anything outside ourselves to be attractive and beautiful.

Let us not hide the beautiful natural self and if we choose to use aids of a cosmetic nature let it be for reasons of novelty and personal pleasure rather than disliking ourselves as we are, trying to impress others.

Another reason people dislike their physical bodies is due to the high levels of stress and toxic material lodged in their tissues. Through the faulty living habits most people indulge in, such as smoking, consuming junk food, alcohol, drugs, along with perceiving an ugly and evil world, the mental and physical toxins build up making their physical body an unhealthy and uncomfortable place to be in. This, coupled with an active death urge, results in many people wanting subconsciously to get their life over with as soon as possible. They do this by abusing their bodies by forming addictions to drugs like caffeine, nicotine, etc. and junk food such as highly processed diets. Learning to care for the physical body makes it feel good to be in and is an act of self love.

As we come to love our physical body, we will naturally want to care for it because it feels so good. We will be attracted to a more natural diet of nutritional foods, pure water and less meat. Drugs and junk food will lessen their hold over us. We will want to eliminate excess weight (which can be an indication of self-rejection) not because we don't accept it, but because it is a health risk and we want to clean up the body, making self-rejection a thing of the past. We will find we will be drawn to getting outdoors more to enjoy the sunshine, the fresh air and will want to participate in healthy exercise. We will find that we want to clean up the body inside and out and begin eliminating the toxins that have built up over the years through our self-rejecting behaviour. Being massaged, fasting and inner body cleansing such as a colonic may seem like a good idea. As we clean it all up, the body will feel good and will become healthy and full of energy. We want to be healthy and generally keep the body attractive because we are important and beautiful and are going to treat the body likewise. To act differently has to be other than self love.

STEP 4: ACCEPTANCE OF OUR INTELLIGENCE

There is a myth that insists that some people are more intelligent than others. It is true that some people use their intelligence more effectively, while the rest of us place too many self-imposed limitations upon ourselves, yet we all have the same potential.

An experiment a few years ago in a public school in the United States revealed the danger of letting outside influences limit a person's expectations for learning achievement. It happened that a teacher was given a list showing the I.Q. test scores of the students of two classes. Of the first class, the actual I.Q. scores had been filled in, but of the second class the list in which the I.Q. figures should have been shown, had been instead filled in with the students' locker numbers. The teacher and the students believed the locker numbers were the actual I.Q.'s. At the end of the year it was found that the students in the first class with correct I.Q. scores had performed better than those with the lower scores. But in the second class, the students with higher locker numbers peformed significantly better than those with lower locker numbers.

If we are told that we are stupid and let ourselves believe it, we will perform accordingly. This false belief will convince others also that we are stupid and they will begin to treat us accordingly. Yet in truth, there is a genius residing in each one of us and we can expect to let its brilliance surface as we clear away our suppressions.

PEOPLE ARE AS INTELLIGENT AS THEY CHOOSE TO BE.

By refusing to compare our own intelligence with anyone elses, we can create our very own standards and can be as intelligent as we like. The happier we make ourselves, the more intelligent we in fact are.

Those areas of learning that we find difficult such as spelling, maths, science etc., have little to do with our intelligence but rather, as a result of the choices made, on where we have been spending our energy and how we have perceived ourselves up until now. By changing how we spend our energy, from watching TV, reading novels etc. to practicing a new learning skill, like spelling, maths etc. we will certainly become more proficient in these skills in time. If we see ourselves as unintelligent because of poor schooling or a lack of education, it is because we are comparing ourselves to others using certain related standards and not our own. It is all to do with the attitude we have towards ourselves.

The key to intelligence and learning is a matter of time, rather than some inborn quality. Research into learning principles and education has shown this, and most students do eventually master each learning task given the time. Those who don't are prevented by their negative attitudes, and certainly not through any deficiency of ability or intelligence. It is an attitude and a belief in one's own abilities that enables some students to move faster than others and the continued practice of such positive attitudes.

We can master any academic or learning skill with enough time and energy if we so choose to. But we may not want to put our time and effort into learning something that doesn't interest us. Rather, learning how to live, love and be happy may be far greater objectives. We all have enough intelligence for everything that is important in this life, and we can improve it merely by choosing to become more so by spending enough time and energy on that objective.

STEP 5: ACCEPTANCE OF OUR EMOTIONS

There is no such thing as a bad emotion. Feelings just ARE. What may be described as negative feelings are those feelings that make us feel separate from others, unlovable, hostile, inadequate, threatened and a host of other potentially uncomfortable emotions. Emotions are just by-products of structures of thought and are just the physcial reaction to certain thought processes taking place in the brain. When we experience an emotion, we have first had a thought which sends a message to the muscles and organs of the body to react in a certain way.

Worry for instance, is an emotion which is the direct result of holding fearful thoughts in the mind. Anger is impossible if we are having peaceful thoughts. Self-hate cannot happen while thoughts of love are filling our thought consciousness. All emotions and feelings are connected to our thoughts and we can change our emotions by changing our thoughts. All emotions are reflections of the mind and negative emotions are the result of conditioned thought patterns. That is why we use rebirthing in cleaning out these habitual patterns of thought which create feelings of a supposedly negative nature.

Even though some feelings appear more pleasant than others, no one feeling is in any way superior or inferior to another. But most people hate themselves because they have more negative feelings than positive ones. This is because their thought patterns are all clogged up with false concepts of who and what they are.

They merely have to understand that whatever feeling they are experiencing is absolutely right and appropriate at that moment. If it is negative as the result of perceiving an unpleasant and hostile world then the message the True Self is trying to send, is that the person is resisting the Truth, and the 'pain' is that resistance. Pain and negative feelings are wonderful because they are warning signals that we are perceiving a perfect situation wrongly and making it wrong by hating it.

Whenever we feel angry, sad, fearful, resentful, embarrassed, inadequate, threatened or whatever, we can consciously breathe into it (the first component of Rebirthing); then focus our full awareness onto the feeling (the second component); accept and love that feeling (the third component); relax our physical body into the feeling (the fourth component); and realize that this feeling is absolutely perfect and appropriate to experience at this precise moment (the fifth component). Then we can watch with interest the whole emotional experience integrate into that of bliss. This is extending the Rebirthing process out from our normal sessions. Eventually, we will be rebirthing ourselves throughout the day as we go about our normal business, and feeling 'great'.

It is our feelings that get us in touch with ourselves and enable us to clean out those negative thought impulses that insist we are bad, unimportant and don't measure up.

By loving our feelings, or at least loving ourselves for having them, we eventually see beyond them and see the hoax being played upon us by the ego.

By seeing this and loving our feelings, we can welcome every feeling as a new experience in the here and now.

STEP 6: ACCEPTANCE OF OUR UNIQUENESS

One of my rebirthing clients taught me a wonderful lesson once. Ricky was a young man in search for himself and was responding excellently to rebirthing by beginning to totally accept himself after years of self-rejecting behaviour. In order to stimulate this growth further, I asked Ricky what it was that he could do better than anyone else. The answer he gave me was one I probably wasn't prepared for.

He said, 'I can be ME better than anyone else in this world'.

This is the total answer to the question of self-doubt. Each of us can be that unique individual self that we are, better than anyone else. Once we learn who we really are by cleaning out the ego, we can begin to enjoy our true self. We are all best at being different and unique.

Some of the most tortured people in the world are those who are continually straining to convince other people that they are someone or something other than what they basically are. Oh, the relief and fulfillment that comes when one finally gives up the pretence and role playing and is willing to be their own unique self.

Love, acceptance and fulfillment are often cut off from us when we strive to be somebody else, and come almost of their own accord, when we relax and be ourselves.

The great Saint Rav Zussye of Tarnifal, just before his death trembled as he thought, ''I am about to face the blessed and Holy one, and justify my sojourn on the world. If he should ask me: 'Zussye, why were you not like Moses?' I shall reply, 'because I was not granted the wisdom you granted Moses'. If He should ask me: 'Zussye, why were you not like Rabbi Akiba?' I shall answer, 'because I was not granted the powers you granted Rabbi Akiba'. But the Almighty will not ask me why I was not like Moses, or why I was not like Rabbi Akiba. The Almighty will ask me: 'Zussye, why were you not like Zussye, why did you not fulfill the potential which was Zussye, and It is for this question that I tremble.''

Every individual that is born is an expression of something that has never existed before, something totally new, original and unique. If there had been someone like us previously, then there would be no need for us to be here. But, being completely different from anyone else ever before or after, it is the task of each of us to discover our own uniqueness and to fulfill our particular unprecedented, never repeating potentialities. 'Self-Realization' is nothing more than the actualisation of our own unique potential and not the imitation of someone else's.

We only ever feel incomplete when we measure our own self-worth against others. Comparisons with others almost always leave us feeling either superior (based on suppressed feelings of inferiority) or frustrated, inadequate and jealous. These ideas which lead us to act accordingly are self put-downs by imagining that we are loved less, or do not measure up by making others more important than ourselves.

With practice in self love and acceptance, any situation where previously we had found ourselves to feel inferior or jealous, can be changed. Through believing so much in our own self-worth, we can appreciate the strengths of others and won't need the approval and love of others to give us value.

STEP 7: ACCEPTANCE OF SELF AS WELL AS OTHERS

Accepting ourselves means also accepting other people who are different from us. It can happen that we meet someone who believes that their way of doing things or their belief is the only 'right' way and that everyone else is wrong. This approach is commonly found with some religious and political ideologies. These people will not accept what we are or have to say but insist that what they say is absolutely true; (which it is for them). These people have built a structure of belief mostly from lessons received from other people, rather than from their own inner experience of self realisation. What can then happen is that if anything is said against this belief, can threaten the structure, and so to preserve it, they close themselves off from different thinking people. If we ourselves are one of these or we run into someone like this and find it hard to accept and love them, then we need to question and examine our own conditioned belief system and the emotional block which is stopping us from loving them. We need to examine closely these feelings of resentment and non-acceptance inside us, because these feelings are telling us that there is a part of ourselves that we are not accepting and is being mirrored in the non-accepting person standing before us. By opening up our heart and accepting that person, we open up an invisible channel of compassion which will do far more to influence them, to look at themselves and broaden their viewpoint, than any attempt in trying to force our ideas on them will ever do. Acceptance and love is unconditional and not dependant upon others thinking and believing as we do. To try and change them by imposing our belief structure is denying their uniqueness and their right to be different from us. Every belief that is without doubt in our minds is our reality, because we all create our own reality. Other people's beliefs are their reality. It may be unreal to us, but to them it is real. The person who has wide views and beliefs, yet does not accept other people because of their beliefs is more limited than the person who has narrow beliefs, but is more accepting within that structure and also accepts the possibility of other ideas as well. Our refusal to accept another person as an important person in our eyes because they are different, is not only denying them as a person, but also is denying a portion of ourselves. And we should always remember:

"Everyone is doing the right thing at the right time in the right place". So we do not have to change anyone. Just accept and love them — that is true unconditional love.

STEP 8: SELF-ACCEPTANCE V. GUILT

Parents, teachers and many adults use guilt as a form of manipulation to motivate others, particularly children, and as a means of control. (eg: you should be ashamed of yourself...). If we have been fed this mental junk then we have been taught to have a poor self-concept right from the start. But worse, not only are we susceptible to being controlled by others through subtle forms of manipulation such as guilt, we are also likely to use it as a weapon against others, possibly our own children. Making others feel guilty in order to get our own way is often very effective, but it is dishonest.

It is dishonest because we are not being straight with a person and telling them exactly how we feel about a particular situation, eg: 'You forgot to put out the garbage again. I guess I'll have to do it with my crook back and all'. (manipulation), or alternatively we can say, 'I feel a bit annoyed that the garbage wasn't put out again. Can we discuss a way round this, to avoid missing the pick-up time?' (assertion).

If we suffer from guilt in any form, then a lack of self-acceptance still lurks within us. Guilt is only possible if we dislike ourselves in some way and therefore we are open to people using that weakness against us to make us feel bad, in order to get us to do something they want.

Feeling guilty will mostly be the results of someone else's demands and expectations. We must understand that we need never live up to anyone else's standards or rules of how things should be done. By loving ourselves, guilt will fall away for ever.

STEP 9: NEVER PLACE ANYONE OR ANYTHING ABOVE OUR OWN SELF

Whenever we regard someone as more important than ourselves, we have just devalued ourselves. There is no difference in giving someone more or less prestige than we would ourselves. Regarding someone higher or lower than ourselves both stem from feelings of inferiority and non-acceptance.

The word 'humility' as I like to apply it, has nothing to do with lowering oneself before another, but rather is about loving all others as one would oneself, certainly not less or more.

There is no institution, corporation, society, organisation etc., in the world that is more important than any human being, no matter how humble or inadequate that human might appear. The cleaner of a large business firm is more important than all the machines, furniture, files, etc. put together. In fact, without the people, no organisation could exist.

We can devote our loyalty and energy to some organisation without it becoming our master, or we its slave. The one thing we need to be totally loyal to is ourselves. But when a club, business, church, hobby, organisation or person demands total allegiance and wants to be regarded as more important than ourselves, then we are being asked to demean ourselves. Organisations should be there to serve humanity rather than people to serve organisations. People are to be loved, whereas things are to be used.

Many unfortunate people can only relate to *things* and find it hard to be with *people* for any length of time. They find talking to people, whose worth is determined by the things that can be acquired from them, a chore.

When we make something or someone our master, we are handing over our responsibility for our own welfare and life to someone else. We have given away our independence in return for so called security or some other benefit, but we are rejecting our inner self.

Hero worship of an individual, or total dedication to some group or organisation above ourselves, is dangerous and we will often find that what we want is unimportant in relation to some urgent task which needs doing in the description of 'one's duty'. Beware of any individual, group or organisation which demands complete loyalty above ourselves, whether it be in the name of learning, task, profits, duty, or some teacher. People and living things are all that matter, and without them, there would be no meaning to life. Life is the only thing that is important and our own life is the most important of all to us.

STEP 10: SELF-ACCEPTANCE WITHOUT COMPLAINT

Self love means accepting ourselves and our world without complaint. Self lovers never complain about whether things are working out or not, if the weather is wet, the rocks are rough, the ice too cold, the hill too steep and so on. Self-acceptance means not complaining about the things for which we can do nothing. Complaining is a useless activity which encourages self-pity and self-rejection and which prevents us from enjoying our present moment. It brings to attention all the negativities in our lives and as our thoughts are creative, we simply create more of what we complain about.

Complaining is used as a prop for people who need approval and reassurance and achieves nothing except our performing in an activity which is self-rejecting.

To complain to anyone is in fact a form of abuse. We are using them as a dumping ground for our neurotic garbage. This is not to say that we should not express how we feel when we need help in some small way or someone is infringing upon our rights. What is being said here is that to complain to someone who is powerless to help us but endures our negativity is straight out unadulterated abuse. What often happens is that they drag out their own kit-bag full of self-rejecting misery and abuse us back with their own complaints. A question that can be asked during such times and which often terminates this behaviour is: 'How can I help you?', or 'Why are you telling me this?'. A question like this enables the complainer to see how useless this type of behaviour really is.

Our response to any experience in our exterior world is a reflection of our inner world. Thus, our complaints directed against anything out there are nothing more than extensions of our inner negativity.

Every experience is a learning experience no matter how painful it may appear at the time. We can either reject the lessons by suppressing them or complain about them or alternatively, we can ask ourselves: 'What can I learn from this?', or 'What is life trying to teach me?'. This approach will short circuit any desire to complain and will provide us with valuable growing experiences.

BILL OF RIGHTS FOR SELF-LOVERS:

1. I have the right to be me — the way I am and the way I want to be.
2. I have the right to think and feel any way I choose, to be the ultimate judge of my actions and be completely responsible for them.
3. I have the right to love whomever I choose and allow myself to be loved in return.
4. I have the right to love and respect myself, to plan, to win and become the very best that I can possibly become so long as I am honest and manipulate no one in doing so.
5. I have the right to change, to grow, to learn about myself and my world, to make mistakes, and be responsible for them.
6. I have the right to say no and be independent of the approval of others.
7. I have the right to privacy, a time to be on my own, to keep a part of my life secret, no matter how important or trivial.
8. I have the right to question anyone in matters that affect my life, to be listened to and taken seriously.
9. I have a right to be trusted and taken at my word. If I am wrong, to be given the chance to make good.
10. I have the right to change my mind, and never give reasons or excuses to justify my actions.
11. I have the right to say I don't know or not to answer questions from those who have no right to ask.
12. I have the right to solve my own problems, to make my own decisions and find my own happiness in the world.

CHAPTER 24

FORGIVENESS

Forgiveness is ceasing from making a Perfect situation wrong. Because we once forgot who we were (love and perfection) we judged someone or something as bad or wrong.

If we truly loved ourselves and everyone else, 'forgiveness' would never be necessary. Forgiveness is only needed after condemnation. Condemnation means blaming others and is based upon the desire to punish. Rather than always focusing on forgiveness, we need to focus more on love, and the purity of non judgement and acceptance. That is the aim. This can only be achieved by being in the present moment and seeing the perfection of everything. However, for most of us, it may be necessary to release the suppressed angers and blame for our perceived 'made wrongs' of the past. For this we need only let go of condemnation, and the desire to hurt someone.

We condemn others with angers and resentments and condemn ourselves with guilt.

When we condemn someone for having done something we perceive as bad or against us in some way, we are taking on energy that will create future mental and physical illnesses.

Any form of resentment or anger against even one other person is a sign of blame for someone. The load of even the smallest suppressed hostility is too heavy for anyone to carry. Bitterness, blaming, and anger are created because that person has passed judgement on the actions of someone else as bad, evil, hurtful, or wrong. Love and Forgiveness cost nothing, but bitterness and blame has a cost that no one can afford.

Authentic Forgiveness is of such vital importance in finding lasting peace and happiness that I call it 'forgiveness therapy'. Rebirthing is all about Forgiveness therapy because we are letting go of the past. Forgiveness is a most valuable tool Rebirthers can work with in releasing their clients from the prison of long standing anger and resentment. True Forgiveness is one of the most important aspects toward self-healing, yet it is surrounded with misunderstanding and confusion as to it's nature. So, to determine what true Forgiveness is and what it means, let us first explore what it is not.

Forgiveness is not acting superior and pardoning sins that we imagine are real. If we believe that someone has broken some rule, 'sinned' in some way, or acted 'wrongly', it is very easy for our ego to assume a position of superiority and show how virtuous we are by Forgiving them. It's like saying: "Bring the guilty 'sinner' in so I can fogive him". Such vanity and 'holier than thou' attitude is just another form of condemnation.

Forgiveness is not suppressing resentment and acting as if everything is alright, while we feel it is not. We may believe that it's easier and safer to brush off the insensitivities, cruelty, and hostile behaviour of others. This may stem from our fear of someone and therefore we can justify our fear and remain in their control by playing the forgiving role. This is the passive role of the 'martyr', which achieves no more than teaching others to mistreat us and reinforces our own self-rejection.

Forgiveness is not when we are motivated to forgive someone out of obligation, because someone has forgiven us and we must do so in return, or because God said we must or some book tells us too. Forgiveness out of obligation is to fail to understand what the nature of forgiveness is. Forgiveness motivated from anything outside ourselves will rarely clean out the deep seated resentments harboured in the subconscious.

Forgiveness is not letting all the prisoners in jail go free, or returning to our ex-lover, or job, or even expressing forgiveness to someone who once crossed us. The ego often believes that to forgive someone who committed an offence against it, means demonstrating some kind of forgiving behaviour. Forgiveness is an internal exercise and while many of us may wish to express our forgiveness in some external way, the true forgiveness is what is taking place within the heart.

Forgiveness is letting go of blame, guilt, anger, unhappiness, intolerance, fears, misery, grievances and a feeling that we missed out on certain things.

Forgiveness is giving up all claims for revenge, and to punish.

Forgiveness is releasing our pent up energy of resentment and fears that block our natural flow of love.

Forgiveness is forgetting all past hurts because they are not worth thinking about as they rob us of Peace.

Forgiveness is an understanding that we are complete and have everything we need and so does everyone else.

Forgiveness is deciding to be happy rather than proving a point; insisting we are right, and that others are wrong.

Forgiveness is the act of looking beyond ego conditioning and superficial motivations of individuals no matter how extreme, and seeing the innocence, love and perfection of them.

Forgiveness means not judging and sees no grounds for condemnation.

Forgiveness is releasing the negative thoughts against the doctor who misdiagnosed an illness causing pain and death to a loved one; against the police department for a false arrest; against our parents for their mistakes; against the person who ripped us off; who attacked us, cheated, robbed, deserted and betrayed us.

Forgiveness is choosing to love. And we are love. To hate and hold a grudge is totally alien to what we are.

Forgiveness is actually dealing with an illusion, because we never forgive anything real, we simply let go of the illusion and misperceptions. Yet Forgiveness is the illusion that reconnects us with Reality. Anger and the desire to punish are not real, but by believing in them makes them real to us.

Refusing to forgive is to avoid responsibility for our own life. Because we create our own reality and the imagined hurts that we have clung to were of our own making.

I Rebirthed a young woman who had been raped by her Father when she was thirteen. Brenda had carried a seething hatred for her Father for eleven years. She distrusted all men, felt socially inadequate even with women and suffered frequently from severe headaches.

On her seventh Rebirthing session Brenda finally integrated the hatred for her Father. She forgave him for all the abuse he had ever put on her in a very intense, tear-filled wonderful session, which also reduced me to tears of joy right along with her.

On her next session we worked on her forgiving herself for harbouring that anger for so long.

The following week, Brenda contacted her Father for the first time in seven years with a letter that said she loved him and wanted to see him again. Her Father did not respond and over the next two sessions we worked through her disappointment. But what was interesting, was that her distrust of men left her; she felt more confident socialising and no longer suffered from the headaches. I last heard from Brenda twelve months later, that she had seen her Father and a warm friendship had developed and that she was getting married.

When we finally let go of our resentments once and for all, we will feel as though a great burden has lifted from our shoulders. Hostility towards anyone, not only stops us growing, but also causes us to contract within ourselves, limiting our happiness and life.

Forgiveness is completed in two stages:

1. Forgiving someone we feel angry towards.
2. Forgiving ourselves for feeling guilty for the so called wrongs against others.

When we let go of all our resentments we will find true and everlasting Peace.

EXCERCISE FOR FORGIVENESS

Make a list of all the people in your life who you don't feel at peace with. Even the smallest resentment is an indication of hate which needs healing.

The list could include parents, step-parents, grandparents, spouse, lovers, children, teachers, doctors, etc. Whether they are alive or dead or no longer in our life, the act of forgiveness not only releases us from the burden of anger etc., towards them, but also will influence their 'being' whatever or wherever they are.

Select one person from your list who you are most angry with or whom you would find it the hardest to say 'I love you'. Visualise their face and the action that we imagined hurt us. Now remember if possible something good that this person did for us. See that their actions were not maliciously against us but simply cries for help. Now, talk to this person in our minds, something like this: 'I want to release the anger I have towards you and free myself and you from these old negative thoughts and feelings. I want you to know that I genuinely forgive you for everything you did or didn't do that I judged was wrong. Because of my fear and anger, I blamed you for what has happened. I now forgive you and release you from all my imagined hurts and grievances. I let go of all the times I acted hurt and believed it was all your fault. I realise now that no one else can hurt me and all my resentments were self-imposed and were aimed to hurt and punish you. I choose to feel only love towards you everytime I see or think of you. I love you, and wish you all the very best in life; happiness, health, prosperity, and peace. I totally forgive and forget every thought that ever seperated us from loving each other.'

Now work on a forgiveness affirmation in this manner:
I forgive...(name)...for...(reason for being angry)...
This or a similar affirmation, written consistently along with regular Rebirthing sessions will free us from a great percentage of all that binds us. Be prepared for miracles, for forgiveness is the great healer.

CHAPTER 25

SELF-RESPONSIBILITY

Growth is only possible when we accept complete responsibility for everything in our lives. Every experience is our own doing. Every thought, feeling, action, and response to the people and events that enter our experience is our creation. This is completely opposite to 'blaming' others or even ourselves for things that happen to us. Responsibility is not blame, but rather an ability to respond as a total human being for our highest good. Blame is a concealed way of communicating resentment and so long as the resentment is concealed, we are unaware of it, which prevents us from responding as we choose.

SELF-RESPONSIBILITY is taking charge of our own life and living it the way we really want to, independent of how others or society says we should. To live it the way we would like to could mean doing the things we really want to do, irrespective of any disapproval we might receive along the way. To live, be ourselves, enjoy and love is all that matters. This is the essence of life and failure to realise this truth can result in getting bogged down with unimportant details of so-called responsibilities, collecting material possessions, having enough emotional security and living the way others want us to. Considering that our life is all we really have, at least it should be pleasing to us.

How do we do this? There is nothing complicated about it. We simply start. We start living as we like by ceasing to involve ourselves with activities and people we don't find fulfilling. Our deeper nature tells us the things we do from a false sense of duty, false loyalty, public pressure and from trying to please manipulative people so that they will like us more.

Living as we like simply means no longer living as we dislike. It doesn't mean trying to make the people in our lives treat us differently, striking out at others we think are keeping us down, or rebelling against social rules etc. It means looking carefully at our own mental chains; seeing how we mechanically live our lives to the 'drum beat' of others. By seeing how mechanical we are in trying to please others ahead of ourselves, we will see, probably for the first time why our life is so unhappy.

People live frustrated lives because they wrongly assume that they *need* other people and that to be loved and accepted, they must conform to the wishes of others.

No-one outside of ourselves is a problem to us. No situation or circumstance is a problem to us. We are the problem to ourselves by assuming we are subjected to prohibitive rules. There are no restrictive rules in living as we like and having freedom; only a false belief in them.

To start living as we like, we must rise up and declare to ourselves with all our strength: 'I will no longer live this frustrating way any longer and regardless of what happens to me, I will take full responsibility for my own life and live it as I choose.'

This is Self-responsibility and while we respect outside authority, particularly the rights of others, we become our own authority. We are in charge and in the driver's seat of our own life.

But, too much independence may just be a way of avoiding close relationships. This so-called independence may actually stem from an inability to trust ourselves to another person. To become close to someone may risk being let down or deserted. Behaviour like this is often the result of previous 'painful' experiences with others, of losing someone we were emotionally dependent on. In an attempt to survive such experiences we wall ourselves off, not wanting to risk a repetition. To become uninvolved and keep our distance removes us from life, love and truth and creates an isolation that helps us avoid growth and change.

The opposite situation is when we, out of feelings of duty or need, allow others to make high and repeated demands on our time and energy. The initial satisfaction of being a helper soon passes and we can feel drained, restricted and controlled.

Self-responsibility is the ability and the willingness to be closely involved and co-operative with others without compromising our own self-respect, integrity and individuality. It is controlling our own life, making our own decisions based upon our own values, finding our own happiness in the world and allowing others the same right.

While Self-responsibility means freedom from dependency on other people, it also means close involvement and co-operation with them. No-one can become totally independent because all relationships involve other people. Doing, sharing, helping, giving and receiving are the roots of human companionship and the very young, the sick and the very old are all dependent on others in some way. 'No man is an island', but at times, we do make very good peninsulas.

Self-responsibility is freedom from the erroneous belief that others can control or hurt us in some way or that our happiness is dependent upon someone else.

We create our own reality, and Self-responsibility is taking charge for our own thoughts, feelings and actions and gives us the ability to stand on our own two feet.

When we talk about dependency, we are not discussing physical dependency but a psychological disorder called 'emotional dependency.

EMOTIONAL DEPENDENCY

Emotional dependency is believing that we need others or someone for our continued existence or happiness. It is when we have assigned our lives, fulfilment, growth and happiness into the hands of some dominant person.

We know when we are emotionally dependent if we:

- feel either happy or hurt based on what others say, think, feel, or do.
- feel depressed or suicidal after the death of a loved one or at the end of a relationship.
- always ask permission for anything, including permission to speak and to do certain things.
- feel duty-bound to visit parents, entertain relatives, have sex, fulfill certain roles and so on, rather than freely choose to.
- allow or seek someone else to make our decisions for us.
- always need lots of approval.
- believe that our happiness is created by other people or persons and that if they were to leave us, our life would collapse; so we are bound to that person out of fear of loss.
- believe that others can control or hurt us in some way.

DEPENDENCY AND CHILDREN

New born babies and young children are physically and emotionally dependent on loving parents and they need total acceptance and lots of approval right from the start if they are to grow mentally, emotionally, spiritually and even physically.

Each new soul on the earth has a tremendous potential which includes the ability to love. But it needs the unconditional love and acceptance of a parent to open the door to all that potential.

In children's growth, their number one emotional need is to find their own love centre and develop their own beautiful self-concept. In finding this love in themselves, they quickly develop and eventually mature into happy, loving, and self-reliant adults.

When approval is given only as a reward, then the love is conditional and the child's growth is stunted, often resulting in later self-rejection, guilt, anxiety and emotional dependency. We can teach our children Self-responsibility from day one by giving them total unconditional approval, acceptance and love right from the start.

To find unconditional love and acceptance in the world, we need to find the love in ourselves first. Then by reaching out we will find it in others.

If we have been denied love from our beginning, then we may find it hard to relate to others on the level of love and so we fear close relationships. The prisons are full of people who had not been exposed to enough love while they were developing their own self-concept.

All humans desire independence from an early age but many parents find it hard to let their children go as they grow up. This is because they think they own their children and that they raise them to hang on to them.

Kahlil Gibran wrote in 'The Prophet':

"Your children are not your children.
They are the sons and daughters of life's longing for itself.
They come through you but not from you,
and though they are with you yet they belong not to you.
You may give them your love but not your thoughts,
for they have their own thoughts.
You may house their bodies but not their souls,
for their souls dwell in the house of tomorrow,
which you cannot visit, not even in your dreams."

All children do really want to learn Self-responsibility as they grow up. But in spite of most parents' good intentions for their children they teach them in many cases, emotional dependency, because they themselves are walking models of emotional dependency.

We cannot give our children self-love, self-responsibility, unconditional happiness, self-awareness, courage, honesty, freedom, inner peace, and self-confidence. They acquire these by first seeing their models, their parents (us), living this way ourselves, and then by their own development.

Most parents want to see their children fulfilled and happy and to ensure such an outcome the parents themselves must be that same way.

If we model any form of self-rejection and non-acceptance, then our children will adopt the same attitudes for themselves. Until we clean up our act of dependency, we cannot be effective models for our children.

LOVE RELATIONSHIPS

In a love relationship and marriage there is a certain amount of physical and emotional co-operation between couples which is normal and healthy, as long as it is based on *choice* rather than *need*. When we need a certain relationship we are externally controlled and will experience anxiety unless our addictive need is satisfied. We know we have an addiction within a relationship when obligations, demands and expectations creep into it. When this happens, choice goes out the window and so does unconditional love. Any alliance where one or both partners feel obligated to be something, or forced to conduct themselves in a manner they would not have chosen for themselves, will not be a happy one. Yet it is not the relationship that is the problem but rather the expectations within it. If we expect or need someone to act a certain way, to watch over us, control us, make our decisions for us, try to make us happy, then when they don't, we experience our unsatisfied addictive demand and the loss of happiness. Expectations promote guilt, resentment and dependency, while choice creates love, happiness and Self-responsibility.

An emotional involvement with someone, if based on choice rather than need, will be an association of two people who love each other to the extent that neither would expect the other to be or do something they would not choose for themselves.

The more we need a certain relationship, the more vulnerable we are to be manipulated and exploited.

Let us not confuse needing others with wanting others. Wanting others, desiring approval and love is one of the strongest human drives. But if we experience unhappiness or collapse when we don't get it, then it is a need and an addiction. Also let us not confuse *not* wanting others with Self-responsibility. Not wanting others can be as unhealthy as the other end of the scale in needing others. Not wanting others may be just a way of avoiding close relationships and withholding love.

We remain dependent for a number of reasons, and even when we know that we are dependent, we remain so. The reasons are:

1. To keep us in the protective care of others, making us feel safe.
2. To avoid taking responsibility for our actions, thoughts and feelings and remain secure in our reliance on others who will be responsible for us.
3. We have a ready excuse to explain our shortcomings because after all, we are not responsible for them.
4. We think it's easier for others to make us happy rather than having to do it for ourselves.
5. We can avoid the risk and work needed for change and growth.
6. We can feel good about ourselves because we are pleasing others who want us to stay in this dependent role and dominate us.
7. We want someone else to make those difficult decisions for us.
8. Because we have been conditioned into being dependent by parents and teachers who never taught us Self-Responsibility.

Being internally secure is also being aware of the numerous forces and attractions in our external world. We are bombarded with outside influences every minute of the day. Advertising, television, the seasons, the weather, karma, the stars, other people's vibrations, and internally by our own conditioning from the past, which all exert pressure. But that is all they are — influences, upon the ego, and even though they may be strong we have the power to ride above them all. But if we believe in luck, or fate, and that our life is already mapped out for us in advance, then we are in the externally controlled area and are most likely filled with all the rules that limit us and keep us on our mapped out route of life.

Being controlled by external influences limits our Self-fulfillment and happiness. When we realise that problems (which are only unanswered questions) are a human condition, and that our aim is not so much to eliminate them, but to cope with them, then we can accept full responsibility for everything we experience. Internal security is where we trust ourselves to handle anything that may come along. This is the security that will never let us down. We can lose all our possessions and money through unforseen circumstances. Those we love and trust can desert us or die. We can lose our job or position through a miscalculation, but we can believe so much in ourselves and our internal strength, that no matter what is happening outside and around us, we remain calm and centred.

Self-responsibility is a security which can be redefined as allowing us to be effective in dealing with our inner world without the need for 'external security'.

Finding true security means taking charge of ourselves and living how we choose to and not the way others say we should.

BUILDING SELF-RESPONSIBILITY

The following are some steps that will develop Self-responsibility.

1. DECLARING OUR INDEPENDENCE

Make a list of everything in our lives that we are emotionally dependent upon. The list could include alcohol, cigarettes, drugs, needing approval and love from a certain person etc. Be specific and detailed in the list.

Let's set a goal to eliminate all those areas where we are dependent in some way. Then if we participate in a function or area that we were previously dependent upon, it will be done out of choice and not a need.

A good affirmation to use: 'Today I declare my independence from the emotional need of others and take full responsibility for my own thoughts, feelings and actions'.

2. COMMUNICATING WITH THE DOMINANT PERSONS IN OUR LIVES

Talk with each person who dominates us or those we feel psychologically dependent upon. Declare our wish to sometimes function independently. At a time when we feel unthreatened, explain to them that we sometimes feel manipulated, obligated and submissive. That the feelings are ours and that there is no blame directed at them. This will tend to make them receptive to what we are saying, because they will not feel threatened. If there is to be any honesty with those in our lives, we need to express our feelings of obligation and submission. Feelings of submission are often based on fear. But we must never consent to a human relationship based on fear. This does not mean that we necessarily end the relationship, but to end the fear in it. Take these four steps:

a) Think of someone whom we fear in one way or another. (We must

honestly admit the fear, otherwise nothing can be done). We can use this following experience in building new courage toward everyone.
b) Act and think and speak toward this person in the way we would if they were an equal (which they really are). Do not mentally submit to him or her. Crack our usual behaviour pattern. Dare to offend him with our new independance. It is absolutely necessary that we dare risk offending him. We are afraid because we don't want him to get mad at us. RISK IT! Let him get mad if he wants to. But assert oneself in very small ways at first. If we take too much at one time we may not be able to make ourselves do it.
c) As we 'play up' in their eyes, keep ourselves emotionally un-involved with whatever happens. Stand aside and observe the reactions and results, both within ourselves and in the situation. Watch whatever occurs with an air of indifference to consequences.
d) Persistent practice will give us a new sense of independence, which, incidentally, we had all along but didn't realise it. Now, with awareness of our natural freedom, we can enjoy it. And we won't be afraid of any other human being on the face of the earth.

As we do all this, we will observe a definite change in our attitudes and actions toward others. We will realise that we are genuinely independent. We are not afraid of offending them as we used to be. We are free of the awfully anxious thought that they might leave us, or not like us any more. We control them in an entirely new way, through no control whatsoever. We let them behave as they wish, while we keep our peace whatever their behaviour. To be free of other people, to be free from the erroneous belief that others can hurt us in some way. That is the goal. And that is the basis of authentic compassion, for freedom from fear of others provides the true ability to love them.

3. INSISTANCE ON FINANCIAL INDEPENDENCE

We are dependent if we must ask for money and rely on the good will of someone to provide us with our financial needs. If this is impossible arrange to earn our own money in any creative way we can devise. Insist on financial independence with no strings and no accounting to anyone.

4. NON-RESPONSIBILITY TOWARDS THE HAPPINESS OF OTHERS

It is important to realise that we have no responsibility to make another living soul happy except ourselves. It is true that one of the real joys in life is helping others to be happy, providing situations where they will experience joy. But others make themselves happy. Therefore, we may enjoy the company of another, but if we feel it is our mission to make them happy, then we are likely to also feel gloom when they are down. Or even worse, we may feel as though we let them down.

We are responsible for our own emotions and so is everyone else. But if we try to control the feelings of another, we can make them dependent upon us.

Furthermore, we must never take responsibility for another's mistake. And we must never sentimentally excuse it, any more than we would excuse our own mistakes. A false sense of love or loyalty on our part robs the other person of the important learning process. Even if the other person refuses to learn the lesson, that is his responsibility. This may seem harsh, but it is an act of compassion. Even Christ refused to take responsibility for those who rejected his message.

5. LIVING INDEPENDENTLY THROUGH LOVE AND TRUST

Allow our partners to do things on their own and expect the same right. At a function, don't feel responsible to be with your partner at all times. Mingle separately and we will meet more people and learn more. If we want to go and play golf while our partner wants to go and see a friend then do it that way! Allow ourselves more separateness and our moments of togetherness will be happier and more exciting. We will feel more strongly toward our partners when we are together and we will treasure our independent activities as well. DESIRE FOR SEPARATENESS IS ONLY DANGEROUS WHEN IT REPLACES DESIRE FOR TOGETHERNESS.

Acknowledge our desire for privacy and not having to share everything we feel and experience with someone. If we feel we must share everything, then we are without choice and feel duty-bound. But above all, let others go their own way and expect this same treatment from them.

The business of living effectively is Self-Responsibility and independence. While there can be real fear about moving away from emotional dependency within relationships, we may be surprised to learn that people most admire those who assume full responsibility for their own thinking and actions. It is interesting to note that we get the most respect for being our own person, especially from those who are trying to keep us subordinate.

Remember these words:
      "Don't walk in front of me, for I may not follow,
      Don't walk behind me, for I may not lead,
      Just walk beside me and be my friend."

CHAPTER 26

SELF-EXPRESSION

Self-Expression in the context that is written here is the ability to say how we feel and think and act without feeling bad, anxious or fearful. It is the ability to be assertive in the running of our own lives and overcoming timidity that makes us non-assertive.

Non-assertiveness is based more on habit than on fear, although fear is probably where it began, and is a form of self-rejecting behaviour. It manifests as the following:

1. Not being able to say no to our parents, spouse or friends without making excuses or feeling guilty or bad, and being unable to express our feelings about it.
2. Being coerced into doing something for someone and feeling resentful about it but not saying anything.
3. Being motivated to do or not to do something by someone else who uses manipulation as a ploy to make us feel guilty or bad if we don't do it. 'Oh, don't you worry about me. You just go ahead and enjoy yourself at the movies. I'll manage somehow to struggle around this house with my bad leg.'
4. Feeling the need to always having to give reasons, or make excuses to justify our behaviour.
5. Not expressing how we feel to avoid strife and conflict.
6. Feeling nervous or guilty when someone disapproves of us.
7. Frightened of not being accepted and liked by a certain group, or individual.
8. Asking permission to speak or do things.
9. We find ourself just 'going along' with what our friends or family want to do and resenting it.
10. Always picking up and cleaning up after others or running our

life on their schedule.

11. Avoid telling someone with 'status' how we feel when they have let us down.

12. Being super-sensitive to other people's criticism directed at us by feeling anxious, nervous or guilty, and responding with defensive counter criticism.

13. Feeling inferior, anxious or guilty whenever we make a mistake.

14. Feeling ignorant and anxious whenever we don't understand when someone is trying to explain something to us.

15. Avoid starting a conversation at a party with a stranger next to us.

16. Not wanting to take a faulty article back to the shop where we purchased it from for fear that the shopkeeper will disapprove of us, or convince us against our will to keep it. Either way we feel resentful.

17. Buying something we don't need from a pushy salesman because we are too frightened to be assertive and say no.

18. 'Just paying the bill' without challenge even though we believe we have been overcharged.

It is not so much the behaviour of being non-assertive that is counter-productive in living effectively, but rather the negative emotions that we feel as a result of being non-assertive which keeps us from reaching out, taking risks and expressing ourselves..

In being non-assertive we tend to become victims of manipulation by other people. Manipulation in this context is a behaviour that motivates us into doing what some other person wants us to do by trying to make us feel anxious, nervous, ignorant or guilty.

(a) "How come you are always working on that stupid car?" (Implying that it is somehow wrong for us to be working on our car).

(b) "Pam's mother lets her. Why can't I go?" (As if to say that Pam's mother is a better mother than we are.)

(c) Don't you care that the rest of the street has signed this important petition and you won't?" (Implying that you are a non-caring person.)

(d) "You should be ashamed of yourself" (Inducing guilt for something we have done or failed to do.)

Manipulation is dishonest because it's playing a power game with other people's feelings in order to get what we want. But many of us use it every day because it works in controlling others and other people use it against us for the same reason. It's that funny feeling we get after someone has manoeuvred us into doing something we would not have chosen for ourselves.

We may manipulate others as a result of not being open and honest with how we feel about things. We try to make others feel bad in order to get what we want from them. We will be more effective and honest if we simply ask for what we wanted.

If we lack self-confidence, then we may have learned manipulative behaviour from people (possibly from our parents) who used it on us successfully as a weapon to make us behave, and so we may have adopted it for ourselves to control others. Often manipulating behaviour works best on people who are manipulative themselves and you don't have to look far to see groups of friends and family circles who use this insidious behaviour of kicking other people's feelings around in order to get their needs met as 'normal'.

If we are stuck in this manipulating game trip, we can break this vicious cycle by refusing to play it anymore by loving ourselves enough and learning new behaviour which promotes self-respect and respect for others.

There are four basic behaviours relating to assertiveness:
1. Passive behaviour;
2. Indirect behaviour;
3. Aggressive behaviour;
4. Assertive behaviour.

PASSIVE BEHAVIOUR:

This is where we allow ourselves to be manipulated, pushed around, demeaned or put down by others and react by being apologetic or some other inappropriate self-put-down behaviour. It is letting others make decisions for us; being too shy to express our feelings or opinions; denying our own rights; avoiding disapproval and conflict at all costs; allowing others or even wanting others to control us. Passive behaviour is fearing what others can do to us and doing little about it except feeling frustrated, resentful and anxious. So we virtually become a doormat for other people, not so much that they want to hurt us, but because they don't notice us. Our sitting back, feeling angry inside but too frightened to express how we feel is interpreted by others as our agreement to what they are saying or doing. Passive behaviour comes from self-rejection, which teaches others to treat us the same way.

INDIRECT BEHAVIOUR:

Indirect behaviour is pretending and making up excuses to get what we want. It is expressing wants through 'pussy footing' around and in round-about actions and words. It is being too diplomatic to the point of being dishonest to avoid hurting other people's feelings. It is a form of game playing and expecting others to second guess our feelings and opinions and so the risk of being misunderstood is very high. Indirect people find it almost impossible to say no and mean it.

AGGRESSIVE BEHAVIOUR:

Many people confuse aggressive behaviour with being assertive. Aggressiveness is not assertive behaviour. It is 'foot stamping', hostile behaviour that demands others to do things our way.

Aggressive behaviour is expressing wants and opinions in a way that manipulates, demeans or 'puts down' ideas, feelings and rights of other people.

Aggressive people over-react to situations with physical or verbal violence in the need to dominate passive personalities. They are intolerant of defeat and weaknesses in themselves as well as in others and try to succeed through power games.

Sometimes, after bottling things up over a period of time, a passive person explodes into an avalanche of aggressive behaviour.

ASSERTIVE BEHAVIOUR:

Assertive behaviour is when we express our opinions, feelings, wants and ideas clearly and directly without feeling guilty, ignorant, anxious, hostile or apologetic, and repeating them even when under pressure from other people who insist or imply we are wrong. We feel self-confident enough to stand up for our feelings, ideas and our rights without putting anyone else down. It is being totally honest without being needlessly hurtful or violating other people's rights. It is stating our position and rights and acting on our beliefs without feeling the need to justify, give excuses or reasons for our behaviour. It is a behaviour that takes full responsibility for our feelings, thoughts and actions in solving our own problems and finding our own happiness.

The key to self-assertion lies in expressing how we feel about a certain situation rather than about the people involved. We direct our comments onto our feelings; for example:

"I feel pissed off when you smoke in bed." Rather than,

"You piss me off when you smoke in bed."

The basis behind the first statement which appears to be saying the same thing, is saying — "I am responsible for my feelings and I have chosen to feel upset right now. I am not asking you to change your behaviour but I'm letting you know how I feel when you behave in a certain way." You have offered the choice of continuing the behaviour, to change or settle on a workable compromise. The second statement says: "You are responsible for me feeling this way and should change so I can feel better."

The first approach may need to be explained to a friend, spouse etc. in order to get our message across.

If we remember to stay in the "I feel (emotion) because...", rather than "You are an idiot, because...", there is less likelihood of creating barriers between you and who you are inter-relating to, with more choices of improving communication.

But the main point about assertive behaviour which many people overlook, is the ultimate objective of self-assertion and the attitude which relates to it. It seems that most people learn to become self assertive in order to be more effective in getting their needs and wants met. Some even learn it to get 'even' or hit back at a world they conceive to be cruel and hostile, or at least gain some measure of control over it and many of the people in it. Some even learn it to be more effective in manipulating others and to increase self profit. But all this only reinforces the ego and keeps us trapped in our addictions and sometimes separate us from one another. The object of self-assertion tuition as well as most self-improvement techniques, it seems, is to enhance an ego that is not accepting itself. Most people learn self-improvement because they are not accepting fully the way they are. Total self-acceptance is the greatest ability and only self-improvement we need. So it is an attitude we need to focus on rather than a behaviour.

Thus, the compassionate attitude to self-assertive training is to develop the ability to be caring, loving and understanding of other people's points of view, while clearly presenting our own.

CHAPTER 27

GENERAL HEALTH

Rebirthing is effective on everyone, no matter what the state of their physical, mental or emotional health. However, it has been found through experience that a person in good physical and mental health finds rebirthing easier than someone in poor health. This is because in a healthy person, all energy movements in the body are related to the integration of suppressed energy, whereas a person who has an illness, will find that the patterns of energy activated will often be related to the illness rather than the suppressed energy patterns. Granted, an illness is another form of suppressed energy and rebirthing will work wonders at healing the illness. But to a large degree this will prevent the rebirthee from activating the more subtle suppressed energy patterns thus slightly reducing the overall effectiveness of the process. That is, the main patterns of energy will revolve around the illness rather than on the deeper levels of the subconscious where the main suppressions are.

For this reason, it is advisable that if we want to get the maximum benefit from rebirthing, we do everything possible to maintain excellent health. Practical activities could include:

- NUTRITION — improving health through a more wholesome diet.
- FASTING — purifying the body of toxins built up over the years through faulty diet and counter-productive activities.
- MEDITATION — alternating profound restfulness with normal daily activities to improve the balance of the physical nervous system with our Inner Being.
- TAI-CHI — a meditation in graceful movement to develop poise, relaxation and general well-being.

- YOGA — of the many different types of yoga — each designed to improve an aspect of ones life, the most common being Hatha Yoga for improved physical health.
- WALKING — for improved circulation and general health.
- SUNBATHING — 10 minutes each day for improved health (avoid 3—4 hours in the middle of the day when the ultra-violet rays are at their strongest).
- SPORT — for overall general health — swimming, jogging, tennis, golf, martial arts etc.
- SPECIFIC GROWTH TECHNIQUES — massage, polarity, chanting, metamorphic technique, saunas, etc.

These are just some of the activities we can explore in order to improve our general health and well-being. We don't have to do them all, but simply choose one or more which appeals to us and go and have some fun. Anyone of these will indeed enhance Rebirthing.

CHAPTER 28

WATER REBIRTHING

When a person has gained some experience and confidence in Rebirthing and is able to integrate anything that is activated in a comfortable, easy and effective manner, it is a good idea to experience warm water Rebirthing.

Warm water Rebirthing simulates the birth experience and many people report that their birth trauma is activated during such sessions. Most people find that water Rebirthing tends to accelerate the activation of suppressions, and if the person is skilful at integrating the material that comes up, much more can be achieved. However, if a person is not yet confident with dry Rebirthing, then water Rebirthing could be too intense and uncomfortable for them. That is why the process commences with dry Rebirthing in the presence of a skilled Rebirther who is able to keep the experiences gentle until the Rebirthee has become used to handling the unusual movement of patterns of energy. Once the Rebirthee has become used to integrating material at a subtle level, then water Rebirthing can also be very gentle, and even more effective than dry Rebirthing in some instances.

A possible exception to starting with dry sessions is when a new Rebirthee has little awareness or body feelings. In this case, it might be more advisable to start with water Rebirthing as the intensity of energy that the water seems to generate may be needed for such individuals.

Occasionally, an individual may experience less activation in water Rebirthing than dry sessions. The reason for this is not fully understood, but could possibly be due to the way the material was . suppressed in the first place.

Water Rebirthing can be done in swirl pools, hot tubs, hot springs, swimming pools, and in large bathtubs. It is best when there is plenty of room for the Rebirthee to stretch out while supported by the Rebirther who also has enough room to sit or stand comfortably in the water.

The water temperature should be between 36°c and 39°c (98 — 102°F).

POSITIONS.

There are many different positions for water Rebirthing. As a Rebirther, I start my Rebirthees off floating face down, body slightly curled, breathing through a snorkel. I stand or sit, (depending on the size of the pool) to one side of them supporting their head with one hand and keeping them submerged with the other arm across their back. This position brings their head close to my chest and they can hear my heart beat. This truly simulates the birth experience for them and often activates the birth memory.

This close physical contact between Rebirther and Rebirthee provides moral support, as well as physical support, allowing the Rebirthee to completely relax into the activated feelings, body sensations, thoughts and memories that come up.

Ensure the Rebirthee has nose clamps and ears blocked, possibly with cotton wool, in order to stop water seeping in, and this makes the experience more comfortable.

From half to three quarters of the way through the session, I lay the Rebirthee on his or her back with their body stretched out and just their face out of the water. This is a very relaxing position for them and finishes off a session particularly well. This position also ensures any residue of activated material is integrated and often the Rebirthee will drift off into a little sleep at the end of the session — which is just fine.

COLD WATER REBIRTHING

Some people find that cold water Rebirthing actually activates more suppressed material than warm water Rebirthing does. This is possibly because the cold water activates thoughts and feelings of fear and of dying, where the warm water simulates birth. As we probably have more suppressed fear in us than suppressed birth trauma, cold water has more to work on.

Cold water Rebirthing is best performed after a person has gained confidence with warm water sessions first. The cold water sessions can be just as pleasurable so long as they are kept gentle and luke-warm water rather than cold water used in the first one or two sessions. After the person has gained more experience and confidence in lukewarm water sessions, the water can be gradually made colder with each successive session.

A cold water Rebirthing session begins by conscious connected breathing before entering the water. Keep the breathing gentle and in a relaxed rhythm. After some minutes, gently enter the water very gradually, an inch at a time. This enables us to integrate the fear that the cold water is activating as we slowly immerse our body. If we get in too fast, our body may feel cold and begin to shiver. If this happens, get out of the water, dry off and begin again, but more slowly. By going so slowly, we actually integrate any sensation of being un-comfortable that our conditioning is evoking in the brain as a result of the cold water. The body automatically responds to the slow immersion by providing additional warmth to keep us comfortable.

As we gain confidence with cold water Rebirthing, we will find it a very enjoyable and invigorating experience. It will also enhance our future dry Rebirths, because of the experience of handling and integrating intense fear.

CHAPTER 29

SELF-REBIRTHING

Any technique that is totally dependent upon another person to facilitate its function is limited. The general direction in which growth techniques are moving is away from such dependency.

Therefore, a time must come in a person's rebirthing process when they must begin to take charge of their own development. This might happen after eight sessions. For some it may take as many as twenty sessions or more with a rebirther before they have enough confidence and skill in the technique to easily and comfortably integrate their own energy patterns.

When we are being rebirthed by a Rebirther, we are actually rebirthing ourselves. The role of a Rebirther particularly in the earlier sessions, is mainly that of a trainer and an emotional support. Rebirthing is basically a self-cleansing technique and it is not the Rebirther who achieves results, but the Rebirthee. The nurturing comfort and encouragement from a Rebirther is vital for a newcomer to Rebirthing, until they have gained some confidence and experience in their own process. After a few sessions a new Rebirthee begins to feel more comfortable with the movement of energy through his body and automatically assumes more and more control over his own process. That is why an effective Rebirther does less and less with each session; to encourage the Rebirthee to take charge of what is happening and to assume more and more responsibility.

This type of training permeates into all areas of the rebirthee's life. So at a certain point in the rebirthing process, each person should begin to rebirth themselves, in order to continue the integration of any remaining suppressed energy. It is important that a person begin to work unaided, to break any ties of dependancy that may have formed between Rebirthee and Rebirther. This should be discussed and agreed between them and normally is evident to both parties when the time eventually arrives. No person can grow in the shadow of another any more than a tree can grow in the shadow of another tree.

Although this book can be used as a guide in all the aspects of Rebirthing from beginning to Self-Rebirthing, it is not enough. Rebirthing cannot be learned from a book. It is vital that a beginner be given that necessary guidance and support during the early stages of the process. If you, dear reader are contemplating Rebirthing yourself without the aid of an experienced Rebirther, I strongly urge you not to. Although you will not hurt yourself permanently by going ahead without training, you may find yourself in the middle of an intense suppressed emotional crisis which you may not handle very well. Nothing in Rebirthing is dangerous. However, attempted by someone with some knowledge on the subject received from a book like this, but with no actual experience, can result in some very intense and uncomfortable situations. So find yourself an experienced Rebirther and learn properly. This will make it all so comfortable, effective, and highly enjoyable.

IMPORTANT POINTS IN SELF REBIRTHING

These are the recommended requisites for Rebirthing oneself:
1. The five components of Rebirthing should be thoroughly known, understood, and experienced under guidance.
2. For the average person, at least ten rebirthing sessions should be undertaken with an experienced rebirther before attempting rebirthing yourself.
3. Confidence and comfort with the movement of activated energy patterns and skill in integrating anything that surfaces.
4. Ideally, should have undergone some rebirther training. (An effective rebirther will provide a degree of such training throughout the rebirthee's progress.)

LONELINESS

A very common emotion that surfaces during rebirthing is the experience of loneliness. This is because before we were born there was no sense of being alone in the womb. At birth we experienced separation and aloneness for the first time. At this point almost everyone interprets this aloneness incorrectly — this results in loneliness, which is suppressed.

During rebirthing when we have a caring person present and

loneliness surfaces, we feel safe and it is relatively easy to integrate this activated material. However, when we are rebirthing ourselves, the loneliness can be accentuated and we need to have a fair degree of skill in integrating our own energy.

Up to now we have enjoyed the nurturing care of our Rebirther, but now we are alone, and so the emotion of loneliness can arise quickly, intensely and without warning. Once integrated however we are free of it forever.

LENGTH OF A REBIRTHING SESSION

This can be anything from twenty minutes to a couple of hours. I generally do an hour and sit a clock where I can easily see it and glance at it now and again. When the hour is up I complete any cycle of activated energy by integrating it and then simply rest there for about 10—20 minutes, breathing normally. Often I go into a little sleep which is very refreshing. Sometimes I do a meditation which is also very relaxing. This rest afterwards tends to integrate any residue of activated material and makes me feel just wonderful.

It is very important not to rush the last integration of material, because of pressure of time. Therefore, allow plenty of time to do a Self-rebirthing session, and allow a good half an hour at the end of the scheduled time for completing integration of any material and for a rest period afterwards.

There is a danger of completing a session before something has been totally integrated. This can happen near the end of a session when a pattern of energy has been activated and rather than go through the complete cycle of Breathing, Focusing Awareness, Loving it, and Relaxing, we slip it back into suppression. This can result in feeling a little depressed sometimes for a short while afterwards. This is explained by the fact that every newly activated pattern of energy carries with it the desire to suppress itself again. Because of the fact that we suppressed this very same energy pattern years before, once activated, the old conditioning of unacceptance or fear wants the pattern immediately suppressed again. At this point it is very easy to finish the session, go and eat something, or do something else that we would prefer to do rather than face a part of ourselves we have been avoiding. With experience, we begin to see how easy it is to deceive ourselves into believing we are finished, where in fact we are using an avoidance technique. To integrate any pattern of energy it is necessary to use enough discipline to continue Conscious Connected Breathing instead of following the desire to stop. We know we have finished the session when we feel fantastic and could go on enjoying it forever. If we feel like we would like to finish and do something else, then we are not — and something needs integrating.

I have never heard of anyone who has ever been successful in Rebirthing themselves without first being trained by an experienced Rebirther. However, I have heard of some cases where people have experienced a spontaneous Rebirthing without any training, or even realised what was happening to them. But they were unable to re-create the experience, because generally, they were initially activated by some major crisis in their lives, or they experienced it because the conditions to facilitate the Rebirthing process were just right at that time.

For instance, deep relaxation through long meditation and yoga, can in some circumstances suddenly release suppressed material. Sex has been known to activate energy because of the heavy breathing, (don't laugh, it's true). My ex-wife often went into a full rebirthing session when we made love, and in those days, neither of us knew what the 'hell' was happening, having never heard of Rebirthing. At the point of orgasm the suppressed material would suddenly surface, and for her, it came as emotional grief, which scared the daylights out of both of us. It was not until years later that we learned Rebirthing and understood what had happened.

Rebirthing ourselves enables us to continue a valuable growth process. Effective Rebirthers will train and encourage their clients to learn to Rebirth themselves. However, it may take a little time to break away from the comfort and aid of an experienced Rebirther, and for a while, maybe once a month, it probably is a good idea to have a session with him or her while Rebirthing ourselves once or twice a week. Even years after first learning Self-rebirthing, I often seek out and enjoy a Rebirthing session with associate Rebirthers. This enables me to relax a little more into it, knowing that whatever happens, someone else rather than my own in-built nurturing parent will care for me. This helps me to activate more than I would on my own and thus get through more. But the process works just as well Rebirthing ourselves once we have been properly trained.

CHAPTER 30

LAST WORDS

On first learning Rebirthing, we were probably given a formal definition of what the technique involves — Rebirthing is a personal and growth process, using a breathing technique to clear out physical, mental and emotional blocks and stresses.

We were probably also told that the expansion of consciousness happens as the system becomes clearer, allowing the natural flow of life giving energy to the three main functions of our Being, (the intellect, the emotions and the physical body). I have separated these three functions in order to identify each one independently. In truth, they are not separate, but act as one system, acting in unison for our good and for the good of all humanity. We are whole and complete and have all we need right now. The reason we may not feel this way is because we have separated ourselves from ourselves, by making the loving energies of the universe 'wrong' by suppressing them. This creates the illusion of separation, loneliness, and unhappiness which in turn creates an accumulation of stress that manifests itself as energy blocks in the three functions. By cleaning out these suppressed blocks, we integrate the intellect, the emotions and the physical, which then unites our manifested self with our higher spiritual Self.

The ultimate aim of living is to find our Inner bliss. For this we may need techniques like Rebirthing, which is in my opinion, one of the most effective methods of finding that 'Kingdom of Heaven within'.

Rebirthing is not about teaching anything new. We all have the knowledge of Truth instinctively already. Rebirthing is all about unlearning all the untruths of fear, anger, unhappiness, etc; all the illusions, and letting go all that is false.

Rebirthing training is simply processing patterns of energy that are activated at any time, and not just during a Rebirthing session. During a Rebirthing session, we use Conscious Connected Breathing to activate the suppressions. But in being faced with a supposedly difficult situation such as a family fight, or a confrontation with someone, where once we would have either fallen to pieces, reacted with anger, or suppressed the experience, we can process it right on the spot. We don't need to do anything to activate energy at such times, because we are already activated. The energy from the past suppressions, (our ego and conditioning) have come up, and triggered off the present 'difficult situation'. What a marvelous opportunity to integrate our past 'wrongs' right now, and we can for example:

1. Gently breathe into our anxious feelings. The breathing can be gentle enough so as not to draw attention to ourselves and to what we are doing. The breathing tends to fully activate this particular energy pattern.

2. Focus our full attention on what we are feeling, and in what part of the body we are feeling it. This will speed up activation and begin to integrate the energy. But more importantly, it brings us into the vital 'present moment'. Remember, this is the only moment that exists, and therefore, the most important moment in our entire lives: (TOTAL AWARENESS).

3. Accept what is happening right now as part of something we have created; take responsibility for it; own it, and love it. Love ourselves for feeling the anxiety. Open ourselves up to the whole experience which will allow us to begin to love the person we are confronting: (TOTAL ACCEPTANCE).

4. Relax all our muscles that are not being used and see that there is no threat to our INNER TRUE SELVES.

5. Realise that what is taking place at this precise moment, is completely appropriate, which makes the whole situation perfect. Remember: no feeling, no action, and no person is ever 'wrong'. Only thought forms, which colour the way we perceive things falsely, can ever be wrong. And even the thoughts themselves are not wrong, but simply are being used to hide the Truth. What is happening around us is not important; it is what is happening inside us which determines our response to outside events. 'Everyone is doing the right thing in the right place at the right time'.

By using the five components of Rebirthing, there is no reason to ever feel unhappy again, so long as we remain fully aware. We are able to extend the Rebirthing process into every area of our lives. We can integrate everything as it happens. We can integrate energy from the past by using the five components the moment they arise. Thus we can process negativity while eating a meal, watching T.V., walking along the street, driving a car, talking to someone, or in the middle of a verbal conflict. The five components of Rebirthing give us the tools to not only clean out all 'made wrongs' of the past, but also effectively handle every new and challenging situation we may encounter in the present. THEY WORK, so long as we use them.

The greatest difficulty of course, is in remembering to use them while in the middle of a depression, or captured by our ego and feeling overwhelmingly angry and so on. Yet, with practice of using them at every opportunity to process little annoyances that come up, we will be more likely to use them when the big 'crisis' happens in our lives. If we are being Rebirthed or Rebirthing ourselves regularly, (once a week), and using Affirmations, then we are building positive behaviour habit patterns which will come to our aid when we need them. But more importantly, we are cleaning the system of old conditioning which once forced us to react in a certain negative way. So now, as the mind/body system becomes clearer, our consciousness naturally expands to embrace our 'Inner' flow of compassion, joy, peace and creative expression.

So there we have it! Can Rebirthing give us full Self-Realisation? The answer is yes, but don't believe a word that is written here without trying it. Try Rebirthing for yourselves and prove it, for the only true knowledge that is worth anything is self-verification through actual experience.

Today we have too many teachings and not enough actual experience of Truth. Opinions, dogmas, systems, beliefs, religious teachings, self-improvement techniques and so on, are springing up all over the place, filling a demand of spiritual emptiness in the hearts and minds of Humankind. Even in this 'New Age of Enlightenment', the so called 'Aquarian Age', far too many gullible folk are following 'jazzed up', 'glossed over' and fancy 'new' systems which all promise salvation and enlightenment. And this is fine, for every system of 'self improvement' has something to offer. But we need to be aware that some systems can lead us away from experiencing our feelings or suppressing bodily functions, or inhibiting intellectual exploration and growth. The aim is to be as fully human as possible.

Through Rebirthing, we are able to once again feel, become alive and experience the joys of our youth, living, loving and expressing our Inner Freedom.

Rebirthing is built around the principle of uniting us with the Truth within us; a journey into our Inner Being to the 'Inner Kingdom'. At the same time, we do not mean to set up rebirthing as 'the only way to a grand and glorious future'. There is no one way to 'Self Realisation'. There is only One Truth, but there are many paths. Rebirthing is just one of these paths in which I invite you to tread for a while.

We must never forget that wonderful techniques like Rebirthing and Affirmations are only means to an end. They are not an end in themselves and it is easy to get trapped into making the technique bigger than ourselves. Rebirthing is a wonderful technique, but eventually we must go beyond techniques and taste the very fountainhead of Truth itself. The technique will help get us there faster and then we need only to walk on ahead — unaided and Self-realised.

Blessings
COLIN P. SISSON

THE AUTHOR

Colin Sisson was born in Levin, New Zealand on the 1st of February, 1946. After many years of struggle and striving he one day discovered that success and achievement was self-related and not determined by other people or institutions; that he could be wise, successful and happy simply by being that way, based upon his own standards and not someone else's. He also discovered that nature always takes the line of least resistance, and true happiness and success are based upon the same principles of natural law; that struggle and pain are sometimes part of the discovery of how simple life really is and once discovered, pain has no further value.

With a Christian upbringing, his search for Truth really began as an infantry soldier on the battlefields of South Vietnam during the 1968 Communist TET Offensive. He recorded in his diary at the time: 'It's beginning, not to make sense to me that two groups of human beings set out to destroy each other for no other purpose than gaining some land, natural resources or political and ego-centric power. Surely we are one — all part of the same human race'. But being a highly trained soldier, having trained with the New Zealand Special Air Service (S.A.S.), he carried out his duties efficiently.

After returning from Vietnam, mentally and emotionally exhausted, he took an interest in psychology in order to continue the search for himself, having glimpsed it on occasions through the terrors of modern war. His search led him to study martial arts,

Buddhism, Hindu philosophy, Christian Mysticism, the works of Gurdjieff and the Qabalah. Along the way he was introduced to many natural healing techniques like massage, fasting, counselling, meditation, yoga and eventually REBIRTHING. He says that while REBIRTHING may not have been the most important thing he ever learned, it certainly is the 'crowning glory' of all his work so far.

Having first learnt REBIRTHING in 1980, Colin became a professional Rebirther at the beginning of 1983 while living at the Aio Wira Yoga Centre in Auckland, New Zealand. In February, 1984 he opened a REBIRTHING clinic in Mt. Eden, Auckland and is regarded as one of the most effective Rebirthers in Australasia.

Colin is a recipient of the 'Queen's commendation for brave conduct', an outdoors man and meditation teacher, and is currently writing further works on healing and self-development. His experience, knowledge, intuition and compassion is a great inspiration to the rest of us as to what can be accomplished when we begin to discover our True Inner Selves.

Kathryn Richardson

BIBLIOGRAPHY

YOUR RIGHT TO RICHES, By COLIN P. SISSON. Total Press 1986
BREATH OF LIFE, by COLIN P. SISSON. Total Press 1987
YOU CAN HEAL YOUR LIFE, By LOUISE L. HAY. Hay House
HEAL YOUR BODY, By LOUISE L. HAY. Hay House
REBIRTHING — THE SCIENCE OF ENJOYING ALL OF YOUR
LIFE, By PHIL LAUT & JIM LEONARD. Trinity Pub.
LOVING RELATIONSHIPS, By SONDRA RAY. Celestial Arts.
CREATIVE VISUALIZATIONS, By SHAKTI GAWAIN. Whatever
Pub.
SECRETS OF THE INNER SELF, By Dr. DAVID A. PHILLIPS.
Aquarian Books.
THE PROPHET By KAHLIL GIBRAN. William Heinemann Ltd. 1980
THE BREAKTHROUGH GAME By PACO. Total Press 1986.

RECOMMENDED LISTENING

REBIRTHING MADE EASY, COLIN P. SISSON.
YOUR RIGHT TO RICHES, COLIN P. SISSON.
LOVING YOURSELF, LOUISE L. HAY.
WHAT I BELIEVE/DEEP RELAXATION, LOUISE L. HAY.
SELF HEALING, LOUISE L. HAY.
THE FORGIVENESS TAPE, KYLE KING.

NOTES & AFFIRMATIONS